· MICHAEL CUNNINGHAM'S

The Hours

A READER'S GUIDE

TORY YOUNG

CONTINUUM | NEW YORK | LONDON

2003

The Continuum International Publishing Group Inc
370 Lexington Avenue, New York, NY 10017

The Continuum International Publishing Group Ltd
The Tower Building, 11 York Road, London SE1 7NX

www.continuumbooks.com

Printed in the United States of America

Library of Congress Cataloging-in-Publication Data

Young, Tory.
    Michael Cunningham's The hours : a reader's guide / Tory Young.
        p.   cm.—(Continuum contemporaries)
    Includes bibliographical references (p.) and index.
    ISBN 0-8264-1476-1 (alk. paper)
    1. Cunningham, Michael, 1952–Hours.   2. Woolf, Virginia,
1882–1941—In literature.   3. Women in literature.   I. Title.   II.
Series.
PS3553.U484H689   2003
813'.54—dc21   2003008919

For Miriam and Susan

Contents

Acknowledgements

Writing this guide would have been a far less pleasurable task without the assistance I received from the English Department at APU, Cambridge, in granting sabbatical leave; Les Brookes and Richard Canning for their expertise and the generosity with which they offered it; Mark Chutter for his kindness in sourcing reviews of the film; and David Barker for his patience as an editor. I'm grateful to many others for their love and support, especially Alison Ainley, Miriam Lynn, Susan Rosser, Anna Snaith, Vicky Williamson, Ed, Jane and Robert Young.

1

The Novelist

In an interview given as he wrote *The Hours,* Michael Cunningham described the "Mrs. Brown" chapters as "a day in my mother's life" (Richard Canning, *Hear Me Out: Further Conversations with Gay Novelists,* N. pag.). While he is guarded about his life and upbringing, the emotional preoccupation with mother and son relationships in his fiction does suggest an autobiographical undertone. *Land's End: A Walk Through Provincetown* (New York: Crown Journeys, 2002), his most explicitly autobiographical publication, a tender eulogy to Provincetown and its inhabitants, speaks of his adult life rather than childhood. Cunningham first lived in the Cape Cod town as a writer, when he was awarded a residency at the Provincetown Fine Arts Work Center. "P-town" has attracted an impressive array of artists and writers—including Norman Mailer, Stanley Kunitz, Mark Doty—whose work appears in his elegiac guide. This esteemed company of American literati was not a community Cunningham ever anticipated joining; he has spoken of his youthful career as a "slacker" (Reading & Conversation, November 14, 2001, www.lannan.org); "I just wanted to amount to nothing" (Emmanuel S. Nelson (ed.), *Contemporary Gay American Novelists,* p.83). His was a "not especially bookish family," there was "nothing to indicate that he'd grow into a novelist" (Reading & Conversation, November 14, 2001, www.lannan.org).

Cunningham was born on November 6, 1952, in Cincinnati, Ohio, a city Reed Woodhouse has described as "even more conservative and banal than the 'Cleveland' of his most successful novel (*A Home at the End of the World*)" (Nelson, p.83). Before settling in Pasadena, California, the family lived in Chicago and Germany. Although his adolescent ambition was to be a rock star, and he read English at Stanford University because "he didn't know what else to study" (Nelson, p.83), he has spoken of the impact *Mrs. Dalloway* made upon him at High School. He has given an engaging account of his introduction to the canonical author. Hanging out behind the gym smoking, Cunningham, in a bid to impress a girl who was "a figure of authority and romance to me" (CNN.Com, April 8, 1999), spoke admiringly "about the poetry of Leonard Cohen." She took a deep drag of her Marlboro and retorted "but I wonder if you've ever heard of T. S. Eliot or Virginia Woolf" (www.nytimes .com). He headed straight for the library and found only Woolf's 1925 novel. Although he had "no idea what it was about," he recalls the "depth, density, balance and music of those sentences" and, under influence of Woolf's prose, retrospectively marries his musical yearnings with his real achievements in claiming that he wanted to try and do "with language what Jimi Hendrix does with the guitar" (Reading & Conversation, November 14, 2001, www.lannan.org). Admiring Woolf's capacity to find extraordinary and unprecedented beauty in the "outwardly usual," especially with reference to her celebration of London in *Mrs. Dalloway*, in writing *The Hours* Cunningham "wanted to confer a similar kind of benediction on the place I was from" (Reading & Conversation, November 14, 2001, www.lannan.org). However, in emotively portraying his mother as an artist, I would suggest that the benediction conferred is upon her,

upon mothers, and not upon places. His father is notably absent—
even more so than in his fiction—from the publicized details of his
life.

After university Cunningham drifted from San Francisco, to Col-
orado, then Nebraska "with a woman he was in love with" (Nelson,
p.83), followed by a stint as a bartender in Los Angeles, before
spending two years at the University of Iowa Writers' Workshop. In
1980 he "emerged a writer" (Nelson, p.83) and moved to New York
City, latterly also teaching Creative Writing, first at Columbia University and now at Brooklyn College. Still resident in the city, the
success of *The Hours* has enabled the purchase of a house in Provincetown where he fondly imagines retiring with his partner Ken
Corbett: "we imagine ourselves, only half jokingly, as old coots
there, prone to a little more gold jewelry than is absolutely necessary, walking wire-haired dachshunds on leashes down Commercial
Street" (Cunningham, *Land's End*, p.170).

As Reed Woodhouse describes, Cunningham has been a successful but not a prolific writer: "his works seem to have come in two
intense bursts: in 1981–1984 and in 1990–1991" (Nelson, p. 83).
Cunningham himself refers to his "largely unacknowledged" first
novel *Golden States* (New York: Crown, 1981) as "practice" (Canning, N. pag.). With characteristic good humor and self-deprecation,
he details its genesis: having "frittered away" his twenties, he pan-
icked and wrote the book in "about forty-five minutes" in order to
have completed a novel by the time he reached thirty. Although critics are generally in agreement with him that it is the weakest of his
novels, the book, now out of print, commands large sums on the
Internet. Cunningham was not, however, embarrassed to offer his
next two to the public. *A Home at the End of the World* (New York:
Farrar, Straus & Giroux, 1990) was his most successful novel before
The Hours and an excerpt from it appeared as a short story, "Clean
Dreams," in *Wigwag* and two anthologies, *Best American Short Sto-*

ries 1989 (Shannon Ravenel & Margaret Eleanor Atwood (ed.), New York: Houghton Mifflin, 1989) and *Waves: an Anthology of New Gay Fiction* (Ethan Mordden (ed.), New York: Vintage, 1994). An essay about drag culture in New York, "The Slap of Love" (ww.opencity .org), inspired the character of Cassandra in his second novel *Flesh and Blood* (New York: Farrar, Straus and Giroux, 1995). The novels, *Golden States, A Home at the End of the World* and *Flesh and Blood*, all chart the trajectory of male protagonists from unhappy nuclear families to "alternative" family arrangements. As Woodhouse describes and as I shall discuss below "'family' is not a dirty word to [Cunningham], though it may be an ambiguous one" (Nelson, p.85). During the 1990s Cunningham was awarded a Guggenheim Fellowship (1993) and a National Endowment for the Arts Fellowship (1998). In 1999 a short story "Mister Brother" won an O.Henry award.

Never ghettoized under the contestable term of "gay writer"—his novels appear in "Fiction" sections of bookshops not "Gay Fiction"—*The Hours* has seen his reputation and readership expand exponentially. In 1999 it won both the Pulitzer Prize for Fiction and the PEN/Faulkner Award for Fiction. In January 2003, following the release of Stephen Daldry's film adaptation, *The Hours* reached number one in the US Fiction best-seller lists. The phenomenal success of the novel, a book that Cunningham had anticipated would alienate many of his readers—meaning the "end of cute boys coming up to me at the gym, telling me how much they like my work" (Canning, N. pag.) initially felt like a burden to the novelist, for how could any subsequent work live up to this success? It is fitting that exquisite prose of his heartfelt tribute to Provincetown, the place he was first a full-time writer, broke his consequent writer's block so successfully that he is now working on another literary-inspired triptych. Walt Whitman features in each of three novellas, one gothic, one thriller, and one science fiction: "In short, it's another crackpot book" (Canning, N. pag.).

The context of gay fiction: literature and identity

There is little dissent among gay critics about the categorization of Cunningham's novels as "assimilative." In his canon, Reed Woodhouse provides an illuminating delineation of distinct groups of twentieth century gay writing. His "Five Houses of Gay Fiction" are structured around a central core of "ghetto literature"; novels such as Andrew Holleran's *Dancer from the Dance* (1980) and Neil Bartlett's *Ready to Catch Him Should He Fall* (1990) which are written "by, for and about gay men" (Reed Woodhouse, *Unlimited Embrace: A Canon of Gay Fiction, 1945–1995*, pp.1–2). The satellites around this core he terms "closet, proto-ghetto, assimilative, and transgressive" (Woodhouse, p.1). Proto-ghetto literature differs from ghetto because its protagonists lack a gay community but both proto- and ghetto display an "astonishing, sometimes arrogant disregard for the surrounding straight world" (Woodhouse, p.2). Both groups are preceded by "closet" fiction; novels exemplified by James Baldwin's *Giovanni's Room* (1956) that, like the ghetto fictions, saw homosexuality as defining, only "horrifyingly so" (Woodhouse, p.2).

Although Woodhouse's categories refer specifically to literature rather than political or cultural groups, they are still clearly shaped by social events. On June 27, 1969, an unexpected police raid was carried out on a popular gay bar, The Stonewall Inn, in Greenwich Village, New York City. The subsequent unrest lasted five days. The Stonewall riots, as they have come to be known, were a landmark in the history of gay rights, launching a movement for equality, and transforming the oppression of the closet and the externally-imposed ghetto, into calls for pride and action. Prior to that summer there was little public expression of the lives and experiences of gays and lesbians in America. Woodhouse identifies the emergence of two distinct strands of gay fiction post-Stonewall: "assimilative" (homosexual or gay) and "transgressive" (queer). In this (literary) context to be "queer" is to be estranged or marginalized as much as to be homosexual, and Woodhouse locates the wit and the dandy here. He celebrates transgressive fictions thus not only for their radical narratives, the often shocking presentation of "extreme psychological and extreme sexual acts," but for their stylistic flair (Woodhouse, p.3). These novels are unlikely to find a large heterosexual readership. Prime examples from this "house" include Dennis Cooper's novels *Try* (1994), *Closer* (1989), and *Frisk* (1991): frighteningly detached and fetishistic, like others in this group they don't simply ignore but actively "repudiate the straight world" (Woodhouse, p.4). By contrast "assimilative" texts while "well written, were rarely brilliant or witty" (Woodhouse, p.3). Surely because of their tacit appeal to mainstream values—especially of family and monogamy—this group includes some of the best-known and most popular gay fiction in America and Britain, including the novels of Cunningham, David Leavitt (to whom he is often compared) and Armistead Maupin. Their defining feature is not the inclusion of gay characters. Their characters "just happen to be gay," and this is just one aspect of other narratives. Woodhouse thus defines their strength, as located not in the dynamism of their prose, but in their rather wistful "appeal to common humanity" (Woodhouse, p.3). With characteristic barb he describes two exemplary assimilative texts, Cunningham's *A Home at the End of the World*, and Alan Hollinghurst's *The Swimming Pool Library* (1988), as "the sort of book you could give your smart straight friends" (Woodhouse, p.182). We can infer from Woodhouse thus that the "problem" with assimilative texts, is that they are written for a straight and not a gay audience.

David Bergman outlines one compelling and widely-acknowledged explanation as to why assimilation, the appeal to the mainstream, is a concern for gay readers. In the introduction to his analysis of gay literary self-representation he describes the difficulty of "developing" his own sense of gayness:

The child who will become gay conceives his sexual self in isolation. I cannot think of another minority that is without cultural support in childhood. Jewish children, for example, from infancy are brought up with a looming sense of their religious identity just as black children from birth develop a sense of racial identity, or baby girls soon find what it means to be female. But gay children—who have a keen sense of being different—often have nothing and no one to show them what that difference consists of, or how one might integrate that difference into a way of life. (David Bergman, *Gaiety Transfigured: Gay Self-Representation in American Literature*, p.5)

Instead, his understanding of homosexuality, as for so many of his pre-Stonewall generation, was distressingly gleaned from the unhappy legend of Oscar Wilde, or homophobic medical texts depicting his sexuality as a "condition" or an "illness" from which he could and should be "cured." In contrast to heterosexuals for whom examples and depictions of male-female romances, relationships, and domestic arrangements are culturally abundant, gay youths were instead hugely reliant upon literary representations of homosexuality. In its emphasis upon mainstream desires and values, "assimilative" gay literature is therefore criticized for its didactic failure to present "difference." Furthermore, Bergman, Woodhouse and Gregory Woods, in their discussions of assimilative texts, focus upon those in which the gay protagonists tend to be emotionally impotent; their attempts to establish alternative families succeed only temporarily, leaving the gay protagonists isolated and often wretched. The subtext of these plots—the misery of the gay characters—is thus per-

ceived by critics of assimilationism as an affirmation of the heterosexual norm.

Both Bergman and Woodhouse recognize then that the development of gay consciousness, self-understanding and sense of identity
is culturally contingent. The counter arguments to this tacit understanding of fiction as didactic emphasize the historical context in
which the texts are written. One proposes the view that, post-Stonewall, after the emergence of the gay liberation movement, gays and
lesbians are more socially visible and representations of homosexuality in popular culture have become more prevalent. Thus authors
are less obligated to construct gay characters whose lives, relationships and careers are emotionally satisfying for their confused and
isolated youthful readers. However, the negativity or stereotypical
nature of much cultural depiction of homosexuality immediately
limits this assertion. A recent article on the film *The Hours*, for example, heralds the new willingness of straight famous actors to perform gay screen roles after "the film industry's long and inglorious
record of homophobia" (Richard Barrios, "Top Awards set to bury
Hollywood's gay curse," *The Observer*, January 19, 2003, p.21).
However, this celebration is tempered, as Barrios indicates, by the
mere fact that this is a news item. Homosexuality on the screen is
still an issue; "it is as if society is still threatened by it."

The most compelling—and contentious—counter to the term
"assimilative" as a derogatory label is dependent not upon the tardy
cultural movement toward public acceptance of divergent sexuali-
ties, but upon an understanding of developments in theories of sexual identity. Such theories have developed coterminously with the
post-Stonewall gay liberation movement. Michel Foucault's *History
of Sexuality, Volume 1*, first published in English in 1979, was a par-
adigmatic attack upon the fundamentally essentialist view of human
nature and sexuality in which gender, the gendered characteristics
of femininity and masculinity, and sexual preference, are static and

biologically-determined. Instead, Foucault popularized the constructionist viewpoint in which "identity" is perceived as provisional, historically contingent, and socially constructed. This understanding of the relativity of sexuality is rooted in the linguistic theories associated with structuralism which emphasize meaning in language as dependent upon those who use and interpret it. Foucault articulated the rejection of a fixed notion of "gay identity" in favor of an understanding of sexuality as similarly contingent. Instead of the rigid categories which recognize humans as either gay or straight, sexuality is thus understood to be fluid. Therefore the notion of sexual "identity" is seen to repress difference, in homogenizing everyone as belonging to one of two uniform groups, either homo- or hetero-sexual. As a term that expresses "difference" then, "queer" has come to replace the notion of "gay identity." Formerly in circulation as a homophobic insult, this word has been politically and academically reclaimed by those whom it sought to oppress. This in itself is an enactment of the linguistic theories which understand meaning as dependent upon context. Once abusive, in new arenas the word is now defiant and liberating. When Woodhouse—amongst others—sets the group of "queer" writers against the assimilators, he finds the first celebrating difference, and the latter, in their apparent aping of conventional family structures, as sustaining liberal concepts of similarity.

Cunningham writes at a time then when our understanding of sexuality is as a fluid force. But the criticism of his novels as "assimilative" is dependent upon the rigid categorization of novels, authors and audiences. In Woodhouse's reading, audiences are either gay or straight—Cooper writes for gays and Cunningham for "smart" heterosexuals. Should we instead recognize Cunningham's novels as speaking to contemporary notions of sexuality as polymorphous, rather than representing or writing for one heterogeneous gay or straight audience? Cunningham summarizes *The Hours* as "about three women of ambivalent sexuality, one of whom is Virginia Woolf" ("Driving Mrs. Dalloway" *Guardian Unlimited*, November 13, 1999). The three main protagonists of *A Home at the End of the World* are gay Jonathan, straight Clare and the sexually reticent Bobby—Jonathan's lover during adolescence, and father of Clare's child in his twenties—who form a family with three parents. *Flesh and Blood* is also multiply narrated by a family of ten characters of whom three are gay.

Is it only because Cunningham is "gay" that his work is included and debated in histories of gay fiction? Woodhouse himself asks "How 'gay' does a book have to be to fall into the canon?" (Woodhouse, pp.182–3). It would be hard to argue that Cunningham's novels are "queer" as opposed to "assimilative," rather that they agitate for the re-evaluation or abolition of this as a derogatory term. His novels are not centered around gay characters but instead focus on the changing dynamics of families and kinship—the conventional households his protagonists grow up in, and the alternatives they create as adults to replace them. David Leavitt acknowledges this difficulty of writing about homosexuality as an understated fact:

Because heterosexuality is the norm, writers have permission to explore its nuances without raising any eyebrows. To write about gay characters, by contrast, is always, necessarily, to make some sort of "statement" about the fact of being gay. (David Leavitt, "Introduction" to David Leavitt and Mark Mitchell, eds. *The Penguin Book of Gay Short Stories*, p.xxvii)

Any novel with a gay character is ghettoized, even now. Homosexuality remains as much an "issue" in fiction as it does in the film industry.

Ironically it is perhaps Cunningham's "fixation on families" (Canning, N. pag.) that affords his novels a place in the gay canon, not for aping heterosexual society—as Woodhouse charges—but for updating the conflict between gay life and family life staged in much gay fiction post-Stonewall. In *The Hours* Cunningham represents the debate's opposing views—of assimilation and difference—most explicitly through the characters of Mary Krull and Clarissa Vaughan as I shall discuss below. In locating his novels not just post-Stonewall but in the era of AIDS, Cunningham's novels demand a re-evaluation of the fiction termed assimilative. Les Brookes suggests the pejorative view of fiction termed blandly accomodationist is itself a contextually-bound and perhaps outmoded critique. He argues that this fiction can be viewed as radical, an adaptation "to the reality of a changed world: a post-AIDS world, which requires a change in personal and sexual relations; and a post-structuralist world, in which a 'politics of difference' has begun to supplant a 'politics of identity'" (Les Brookes, *Gay Male Writing since Stonewall*, [unpublished PhD thesis], N. pag.). Bergman too cites the importance of locating Cunningham and Leavitt's novels as following "a brief, if golden period between the onset of gay liberation and the AIDS epidemic" (Bergman, p.200). Now gay writers, often those termed the assimilators, are attempting to "forge a mythos of their own which pays homage to the family without reproducing it" (Bergman, p.208).

Formal and thematic development to The Hours

Cunningham and his commentators have tended to differentiate between his earlier novels and *The Hours*: "to me [*A Home at the End of the World* and *Flesh and Blood*] are part of a series. The series is now complete; it's those two books" (Canning, N. pag.). What unites the two is their period of composition, both "were written during the first ten years of the AIDS epidemic, and they're meant to be books for people who are mortally ill" (Canning, N. pag.). They are then the sort of novel Clarissa Vaughan seeks for HIV-positive Evan in *The Hours* when she wants to find "the book of his own life, the book that will locate him, parent him, arm him for the changes" (p.21). But Cunningham's career demarcation might suggest that *The Hours*, a novel imbued with the prose and character of an early-twentieth century British woman writer, Virginia Woolf, would form a stark contrast to these earlier narratives. However, her influence is present in Cunningham's earlier work—especially *Flesh and Blood*—and the themes of family, motherhood, troubled sexuality, the metaphors of domesticity and water, inform all three.

A Home at the End of the World, Cunningham's most celebrated work before *The Hours*, is written in the first-person narratives of Jonathan, Bobby, Alice and Clare. As a child Jonathan is besotted with Bobby, a school friend haunted by the death of Carson, his elder brother. Bobby's mother is grief-stricken and commits suicide while his father sinks deep into alcoholism. Seeking familial comforts, Bobby moves in with Jonathan's parents, Ned and Alice, and forms a close bond with his mother: she teaches him to cook, and against her good judgement, they set up a restaurant together. The restaurant fails and Bobby leaves Cleveland for New York City to join Jonathan and his "roommate," Clare. In her late thirties, Clare had "never meant to get this far in such an unfastened condition" (Cunningham, *A Home*, p.142). She seduces Bobby. They have a child, Rebecca, and eventually form an alternative household in Woodstock with Jonathan. This family replaces the fictional one they enjoyed playing in New York, "the Hendersons," in which Clare acted Mom, Jonathan was Uncle Jonny, a bad influence, while as Junior, Bobby was "a dim-witted Boy Scout type who could be talked into anything" (Cunningham, *A Home*, p.156). At their happiest when aping this American family on the borders of stereotype and deviance: "it was the story we drifted into when we lost interest in our truer, more complicated story [. . .] We preferred a night with the Hendersons to our other entertainments," but without bad uncle Jonny "the Hendersons didn't work" (Cunningham, *A Home*, p.156). After introducing them to Erich, his sexual partner, although hardly his boyfriend, Jonathan disappears, too wretched in his love for both Bobby and Clare to witness them as a couple. And even their ultimate domestic happiness in Woodstock is short-lived as, at the novel's close, Clare takes Rebecca away from the group leaving Bobby and Jonathan to nurse Erich as he dies of AIDS.

As this synopsis—and the novel's title—underlines, *A Home* is a narrative of loss, in which unorthodox relationships are configured as a means of amending past deprivation. This pursuit of satisfying alternative family arrangements dominates Cunningham's fiction. The Woodstock household in *A Home* is, as Bobby records, "not much weirder than any family [. . .] At least we love each other" (Cunningham, *A Home*, p.273). Set against orthodox, socially-sanctioned families which are seen to foster misery, harbor cruelty and violence, it is perhaps what Richard Brown in *The Hours* dreamed of in Wellfleet with Clarissa and Louis. And although in Cunningham's novels such experiments ultimately fail, they at least afford respite, while those who attempt to replicate families within society's licensed bounds are doomed. In *Flesh and Blood*, for example, Susan, sexually abused by her father, is the only of the siblings who "bought the package" marrying Todd, a Yale graduate and lawyer, to live in material wealth but emotional poverty (Cunningham, *Flesh*, p. 415). Observing her in middle age, her brother, Will, sees that "the strain was starting to show. People paid a price for this kind of orderly existence, all this obedience" (Cunningham, *Flesh*, p. 415). It is the strain of performing a socially-imposed role: Cunningham contrasts playful, chosen mimicry, for instance of "the Hendersons," with socially-determined roles—a trope of performance he particularly associates with mothers. Mary in *Flesh*, like Alice in *A Home* and *The Hours'* Laura Brown, is also a victim of marriage, her life amounting to a hollow enactment of conjugal duty and maternity.

But although Cunningham presents families as failing the emotional needs of *all* their members, critics have been especially sensitized to mournful depictions of family life by gay writers:

Increasingly over the past hundred years the reference point of anti-homosexual hostility has not been "religion" or "sin," but "family," and in particular, the roles that men and women are expected to act out in the family. (Jeffrey Weeks, *Coming Out: Homosexual Politics in Britain, from the Nineteenth Century to the Present*, p.5)

In the 1960s Irving Bieber notoriously headed the lasting assertion that the parents of homosexuals were severely emotionally disturbed pinpointing the strong mother / weak father relationship as producing gay sons (*Homosexuality: A Psychoanalytic Study*, 1962). Cunningham's focus upon mothers in his novels led to accusations that he gives credence to this theory. In his analysis of *A Home*, for example, Woodhouse finds him guilty of not overturning "Bieber's etiology of distant father, close-binding mother" (Woodhouse, p.177). On first reading the novel Woodhouse immediately identified its story as a "cliché. The son, rejected by his father, is colonized by his mother: no wonder he becomes gay. It's what I remember reading, tremblingly, in the psychology section of Carnegie Library in Pittsburgh in 1965" (Woodhouse, p.177). But, as I have indicated, and Woodhouse goes on to concede, Cunningham's nuclear families are universally deleterious; he presents a democracy of misery, the homosexual sons are neither the cause of family breakdown, nor do they surmount a higher pinnacle of despair than their parents and siblings. Fathers are unsparing in the misery they dole out to wives, daughters and gay sons alike. The critical attention devoted to the template of Bieber's etiology in *A Home at the End of the World*, imposes a theory of causality between homosexuality and the family as Cunningham's subtext. However, his subject is not that dysfunctional families engender gay sons but that families cause despair. Even those who are not bound by convention, who do not "buy the package," attempt unorthodox families to efface the damage caused by biological ones. The representation of alternative households may be a tacit validation of the monogamous unit, certainly the virtues Cunningham admires above all in his fiction are kindness and commitment; in each of his three main novels characters are judged by their "capacity for devotion." But his parental roles are not gender-determined, in particular, Cunningham presents mothering as a role cherished by some men.

Everyone needs a mother. Some of us get one who loves us enough, who does more or less the right thing. Others of us decide to become the mother we didn't have. (Cunningham, "The Slap of Love," www.opencity.org)

In the early 1990s Cunningham was commissioned by *Vanity Fair* to write a story about members of the drag world who had been made famous by Jennie Livingston's documentary film *Paris is Burning* (1990). Although never published by the magazine—which Cunningham attributes to fear; "they'd been expecting high glam" not "these big middle-aged things in glitter gowns" (Canning, N. pag.)—the resulting short story examines the performativity of family roles from an alternative perspective, one in which those who adopt (biologically-impossible) familial roles are more compassionate than those upon whom they are socially-imposed. "The Slap of Love," eventually featured in *Open City #6* (www.opencity.org), is about Angel Segarra, who became Angie Xtravaganza, told through meetings between Cunningham and an older drag legend, Dorian Corey.

"Though drag hasn't exactly become a middle-American value, it's come a long way since 1980, when Madonna was just another easy girl from Detroit and most gay men wore mustaches and polo shirts" ("The Slap of Love," www.opencity.org): Cunningham describes its genesis from a small band of deceptively waifish Hispanic boys in dresses, to the magnificent balls in which the stars of raucous "Houses"—each presided over by a "Mother"—competed to win prizes for their majestic drag. "The Slap of Love" is a metonymical narrative, charting this trajectory through the story of Angel's transformation to Angie, from boy to transsexual through illegally and haphazardly-administered hormones; from violated child of thirteen siblings to elegant mother of the House of Xtravaganza. Although Dorian's narrative frame allows the tale a disturbing but illuminating pun at its conclusion, the tale's center is the account of Angie's resilient mothering of boys like her who had fled the briefest and cruelest of childhoods. She was prepared to use her fists, if necessary, to reinstate their lost esteem. Unlike the male violence of a father (such as Constantine in *Flesh and Blood*), each of the three acts of violence in "The Slap of Love" leave the reader cheering the transsexuals' ability to maintain a (masculine) strength while wearing the chic-est of dresses. When a brutish punter looking for tricks insulted Hector, Angie's "son," and refused to apologize, Angie's punch left him reeling.

"The Slap of Love" is not a story about camp queens in lurex-threaded, adjectivally-familiar "fabulous" creations—Angie is in fact heralded as the first to win trophies not for her glittering excess but for her vogueishness, her "impeccable taste." The story manifests the heart of Cunningham's preoccupation with family. To define it as relying upon a metaphor of drag—assuming another's dress—as a visual depiction of the distinction between the roles that we choose to play and the roles we are forced to play, is to diminish the importance of the clothes, and to undermine the lifeblood that Angie's mothering generated. Instead those who are actors in this narrative have reason to feel guilt. They are for example, the "straight" men who pay for sex with youthful, powerless members of sexual and ethnic minorities, quick to condemn their prey as "faggots" in the face of rejection.

Angie died of AIDS in 1993 at the age of twenty seven, a "good mother right up to the end [. . .] she seemed to have carved an identity out of a *devotion* so unstinting it borders on the inhuman" ("The Slap of Love," www.opencity.org) [my italics]. But it is Dorian—whom Cunningham met after all—who holds the narrative, providing its astonishing conclusion. And it is Dorian, not Angie, who feeds Cunningham's compulsive depiction of motherhood, as the model for Cassandra in *Flesh and Blood.* Cunningham narrates that as he finished writing the story of Angie, Dorian—the internal narrator—died. Subsequently raiding her wardrobe, her "children" were surprised to discover a mummified body to which a note was pinned: "This poor soul broke into my apartment and I was forced to shoot him" ("The Slap of Love," www.opencity.org). This astounding event was reported in *New York* magazine under the almost unbelievably potent headline "The Drag Queen Had a Mummy in Her Closet." The pun is testimony to Cunningham's perception: he celebrates a past nurturing by the "House" mothers, but now drag culture has become more masculinized; now it is mothering, a female virtue, that has been forced into the closet. In *Flesh and Blood* it is Cassandra, like Dorian, a middle-aged drag queen, who embraces maternal duties with most success, not to say finesse.

Cunningham's 1995 novel is a family saga like *A Home at the End of the World.* Although narrated in the third person the chapters are similarly told from each family member's perspective. The story begins with the marriage of Constantine and Mary, united only in that they belonged to emigrant families (Greece and Italy respectively). They have three children: Susan, Billy and Zoe. Constantine overcomes the impotence of his outsider status by becoming a housing magnate; he cuts every corner and flouts every health law in the construction of shoddy houses. His own home is also a façade; he beats up his son and molests his elder daughter. When they leave home he has an affair with his secretary whom he later marries and is unfaithful to, having paid-for sex in car lots. Despite this catalogue of appalling qualities, Cunningham narrates Constantine as a pathetic rather than hate figure—a quality in his writing that may trouble readers who seek depictions of clearly-inscribed good and evil.

Mary, meanwhile, recedes into a silent emotional impoverishment; she shoplifts petty items and takes tranquilizers when her stifled depression rises up to suffocate her. She later forms her sole and unlikely friendship with Cassandra, her daughter Zoe's drag mother, on the basis of a telephone conversation in which they discuss make-up and hosiery and during which Cassandra does not disclose her gender. Cruising the end of an era of narcotic and sexual freedom, Zoe becomes pregnant and HIV-positive, giving birth to a son, Jamal, who epitomizes the phrase "independent spirit." His beauty inspires an unrequited devotion in Ben, his cousin and Susan's son, who drowns himself in despair over his sexuality. Ben himself was conceived through an adulterous liaison between Susan and the man who tends the trees in her garden—their encounters more sexually fulfilling than those with Todd, her white-collared, right-wing husband. Will begins the process of leaving his past behind when, at university, he gives up his childhood name of Billy. He builds up his body and surprises himself in finding love with Harry, a man who is not ruggedly beautiful but kind and reliable. When Zoe dies, he and Harry share childcare of Jamal with Cassandra until she too falls victim to the plague.

The insertion of a drag mother into the narrative of a closed family unit distinguishes *Flesh and Blood* from *A Home*. Cassandra's wit and glamour enlivens the text and brings something of the city, the outside world, into the narrow misery of the generally friendless family members. (The narrative exclusion of friends—for instance,

Cassandra does not have her own chapters—discloses not only how stifled the family are by their history but seems almost to suggest that their failure at familial roles has prevented them from professional and social achievement in the outside world). But as in "The Slap of Love" Cunningham does not resort to cliché in his inclusion of the camp classic of the drag queen. Such "mothers" are something of a trope in popular gay fiction, often presiding over liberated families of gay men and feisty women. Think for instance of the transsexual Anna Madrigal in Armistead Maupin's *Tales of the City* series: she is a matriarch who inverts the expected norms in encouraging sexual promiscuity and drug taking. (Alice in *A Home* is released from her tedium in emulating such a role, at least by participating in Jonathan and Bobby's dope smoking). But in *Flesh and Blood* Cassandra is a model of conventional maternal care for both Zoe and Jamal, and also instructs Mary in her maternal duties. Privy to the knowledge that Zoe has a life-threatening illness, she requests that Mary make an effort to see her grandson: "I'd like you to spend more time with him [. . .] he should know you better, he may need you someday" (Cunningham, *Flesh*, p.297). Until the lesbian family of *The Hours* Cassandra's imaginative ability to communicate with Jamal is the most positive depiction of maternity in Cunningham's fiction. It's just a shame she has to die.

The most haunting death of *Flesh and Blood*, however, is one that speaks of Woolf; it prefigures her drowning in the prologue to *The Hours*; it borrows her metaphorical style; and it calls to mind the journey at the close of her 1927 novel *To the Lighthouse*. In his distress at his homosexuality, adolescent Ben has become emotionally and morally unmoored. When Jamal rejects his sexual advances, Ben capitalizes upon his grandfather's homophobia and racial prejudice (Jamal's father was black) indicating that his younger cousin is sexually predatory. Ben and Constantine exclude Jamal from their excursion, a voyage during which Ben meditates upon his guilt and his revenge at Jamal. Jamal's own innocence is represented through a symbol from Woolf's novel. Like James's treasuring of a sheep's skull, Jamal finds peculiar beauty in a skeletal gull's wing, an object that repulses others. (In *Land's End* Cunningham describes happiness in finding a sea gull's wing and being able to take it home to a lover who "would not be repelled by its gruesome beauty" (Cunningham, *Land's End*, p. 42)).

The ominous feel of the journey is emphasized through an awareness of the trope of Woolf's *To the Lighthouse*. The conclusion of her novel is a long-anticipated journey to a symbolic destination (the lighthouse) with a feared patriarch (James finally travels with his father). The lighthouse, as a distant monument, symbolizes both desire — best yearned for, extinguished when realized — and the phallus; in *Flesh and Blood* as object of homosexual desire, and in *To the Lighthouse* as representing patriarchal order. In *Land's End* Cunningham describes the Provincetown lighthouse as somewhere he will never visit, for all towns should have a landmark that remains unvisited, close up it would inevitably disappoint with its crumbling façade and peeling paintwork. (Ben should not have visited the object of his desire — he tries to fellate Jamal and the boy resists him.) Mentally depleted Ben chooses to capsize the craft and then to swim and continue swimming into death; "green transparencies opened before him" (Cunningham, *Flesh*, p.441). Like Edna Pontellier in Kate Chopin's *The Awakening* (1899) who also swims out to sea, Ben cannot satisfy his desire and so cannot live. Cunningham's narrative presentation of the episode foreshadows the drowning in *The Hours*; he describes the passage of the bodies of both Ben and Woolf as the current sweeps them until they finally lodge on land. His poetic prose also most closely anticipates *The Hours*: "A sprinkling of small shells had caught in his hair and a circle of translucent white glass, worn smooth as an opal by the water, lay in his open mouth" (Cunningham, *Flesh*, p. 443).

The symbolic gesture that unites all three novels is not of drowning, however, but a repeated scene which depicts the pathos of the maternal role. Each of the mothers strives for domestic perfection. Each is framed in a homely image of confection. In *Flesh and Blood* and *The Hours* Mary and Laura Brown (respectively) endeavor to make the perfect cake, Mary for her daughter's birthday, and Laura for her husband's. As an older version of Laura, Mary has what Laura seeks;

the solace of competence. The sight of [the cake] filled Mary with a satisfaction so simple it seemed, fleetingly, that satisfaction was the fundamental human state, and all extremes of loss and emptiness aberrations. (Cunningham, *Flesh*, p.398)

In pursuit of flawlessness, and not just an expression of the "agonizingly sincere discrepancy between ambition and facility" (p.104) both Mary and Laura throw away the amateurish first cakes they bake and frost. This scene is clearly a potent, perhaps autobiographical, device for Cunningham, encapsulating a mother's desire to channel her maternal love into an embodiment of perfection. But only through reading *The Hours*, through the words Cunningham ascribes to Woolf does the repeated scene's significance emerge. In *The Hours* Cunningham portrays Woolf as haunted by the absence of her own mother (who died when she was thirteen) and deeply troubled by not becoming a mother herself. This sense of absence is a counter to the difficulties experienced by those who are mothers in his fiction. The sustained and repeated spherical imagery of baking, of cups, bowls "with a thin band of white leaves at the rim" (p.75), of cakes is finally signified in *The Hours* through the idealization of the maternal role as imaged by Woolf. Laura Brown's baking is situated after Woolf's memory of her mother's reassurance, her capacity to convey that a broken dish "portended nothing; that the circle of love and forbearance could not be broken; that all were safe" (p.74). Cunningham repeats this image of domesticity, of encompassing security, as his characters continually seek and reprise the role of the mothers they wanted and the mothers that they want to be.

2

The Novel

Introduction: The Hours *and* Mrs. Dalloway

But can a single day in the life of an ordinary woman be made
into enough for a novel? (p.69)

Michael Cunningham has described *The Hours* (1998) as a
"riff" on Virginia Woolf's *Mrs. Dalloway* (1925). In its suggestion of
a known melody reverberating throughout a new score, this musical
definition is more compelling than some of the literary terminol-
ogy—"imitation," "homage"—that critics have used to describe it.
For Cunningham has done more than simply rewrite Woolf's novel.
He has updated it ("Mrs. Dalloway"), inserted Woolf, as author and
character within it ("Mrs. Woolf"), and in the third narrative component embodied her theories of characterization in modern fiction
("Mrs. Brown"). *The Hours* describes a warm June day in the lives
of three "ordinary" women: Virginia Woolf as she writes *Mrs. Dalloway*; Clarissa Vaughan, a New York publisher, whose friend Richard
is dying of AIDS; and Mrs. Brown, a bookish and unhappy housewife, who we come to realize is Richard's mother. Clarissa Vaughan,
like Woolf's eponymous character, is holding a party. The narrative
follows her trajectory through New York's Greenwich Village as she
buys flowers for the gathering, echoing the perambulations of Clarissa Dalloway in London's West End. Clarissa's party is a celebration for Richard who has been awarded a prize for his novel,

apparently a rather Woolfian narrative about her: it "meditates exhaustively on a woman" (p.126). In the narrative of his childhood ("Mrs. Brown"), his mother, Laura Brown, escapes from the confines of domesticity to a hotel room in order to read *Mrs. Dalloway.* Like Woolf's eponymous heroine, Clarissa and Laura experience a kiss which is sexually transgressive, an epiphanic moment that Woolf famously termed a "moment of being." Thus split into three densely interwoven narratives, each told in the present tense—Clarissa's New York at the end of the twentieth century, Woolf's Richmond in 1923, and Laura Brown's Los Angeles in 1949—*The Hours* proclaims that no life is ordinary.

This attempt at the briefest synopsis makes the novel sound studiedly postmodern in its interweaving of biographical and literary fictions: the knowing twenty-first century reader may be alerted to this texture by the epigram from Jorge Luis Borges and the fact that Cunningham kills off both his author characters (one doesn't even survive the prologue) playfully in line with the New Critics' rejection of authorial "intention," "the death of the author" as Roland Barthes so compellingly summarized it. At the back of the book Cunningham provides "A Note on Sources"—biographies, archival material, critical and cultural studies—explicitly directing the reader from the novel to other texts and signposting theoretical issues about the fictionalization of biography and the extent to which biographies themselves transgress generic boundaries between fact and fiction. One cited cultural study by Joseph Boone contemplates the "textual unconscious" of *Mrs. Dalloway* (is it *Ulysses?*) recognizing that no literary text is written in isolation but is created wittingly or otherwise with a nod or a scowl at its peers (Joseph Boone, *Libidinal Currents: Sexuality and the Shaping of Modernism,* p.150). Postmodernism taught that there are no new stories, just endless retellings, and Cunningham's "riff" is a clearly signaled valorization of this.

However, this is not to say that *The Hours* demands demystification or qualification through familiarity with *Mrs. Dalloway*. Rather, the two novels have a symbiotic relationship: arguably each is enhanced by a reading of the other. Mutual re-readings disclose more than a pedantic catalogue of similarities: reading Woolf's novel, criticism and biographies in the light of *The Hours* reveals that many qualities of postmodernism developed from modernist texts. In exploiting these features therefore, Cunningham has not simply refashioned *Mrs. Dalloway* for the zeitgeist but has expanded Woolf's own literary and critical theories. Her fictional prose, for instance, makes conscious reference to other texts. And like Borges's quest for another tiger (in the epigram to Cunningham's novel), her narrative strategy may be told in a phrase from one of her own fictions; "like a vast nest of Chinese boxes all of wrought steel turning ceaselessly one within another" (Woolf, *The Complete Shorter Fiction*, p.95). Through shifting interior monologues, and the meshing of memory and anticipation in each moment of the present, her narrative style represents the inseparability of each human life from other lives—"like a vast nest of Chinese boxes" (ibid.). Cunningham's novel builds on the same narrative strategy demonstrating intertextuality in its widest theoretical sense: showing that fictional narratives, narration, and real life are similarly indivisible. His novel is an exploration—critics would say an appropriation—of Woolf's concerns.

Mrs. Dalloway, set in June 1923, describes a day in the life of Clarissa Dalloway. She is holding a party. In an act of apparent consideration for her servants, she collects the flowers for the gathering herself, and, walking through London, she remembers the parties of her youth. Memories of her decision to marry Richard Dalloway and not Peter Walsh, of her infatuation with the decadent Sally Seton, are recalled, as she pictures Bourton, scene of the parties. As she walks, the thoughts of other pedestrians are embedded in the narrative like overheard conversations, even at times directing it; the narrative point of view is passed along the figures encountered on the street. Their meditations are united by the tolling of Big Ben, whose strokes, heard all over London, punctuate the day. In St. James's Park Clarissa bumps into Hugh Whitmore, who, like her husband has been invited to lunch with Lady Bruton to help her write a campaign letter to *The Times*. Clarissa Dalloway feels diminished by this exclusion from the political world and later finds gratification instead in the Prime Minister's appearance at her party. People in the streets muse on the identity of the passenger in a stately car: the Prime Minister? Or perhaps a member of the royal family? Back at home Peter Walsh turns up unexpectedly from India and tells her that he has fallen in love. Clarissa invites him to the party. Meanwhile Elizabeth, her daughter, goes shopping with the repellent Miss Kilman whose erotic attachment to her is, as Hermione Lee describes it, "repulsive" (Hermione Lee, *Virginia Woolf*, p.161).

Woolf's free indirect narrative style allows characters to express the impact of the lives of strangers upon them. Some of the pedestrians nervously witness the quiet ravings of Septimus Warren Smith and the anxiety of his wife Rezia. Deranged by the death of Evans, his friend and Officer, during the First World War, Septimus's symptoms of shellshock have been derided by stiff-upper-lipped medical practitioners. After a Harley Street consultation with Sir William Bradshaw, Smith throws himself out of the window of his lodging-house, impaling himself on the railings below, rather than face incarceration in one of Bradshaw's homes where "rest" would be enforced upon him. Later Bradshaw, as guest at Clarissa's party, brings the news of this suicide. She finds it somehow sacrificial: her psychic well being is dependent upon Septimus Warren Smith. After a day of uncertainties about her life she experiences a moment of coherent identity in the knowledge of the young man's death: "For there she was" (Woolf, p.255).

In the "Mrs. Dalloway" chapters of *The Hours*, Cunningham mirrors many of Woolf's characters—as well as the structure of *Mrs. Dalloway*—sometimes with humor. Often their names signal their Woolfian predecessors. The rather genital sounding Scrope Purvis, who observes Clarissa Dalloway and finds her "a charming woman" (Woolf, p.4), is replaced in *The Hours* by the resonantly phallic Willie Bass, who admires Clarissa's "certain sexiness" and "good-witch sort of charm" (p.13). Hugh Whitmore with his "extremely handsome, perfectly upholstered body" (Woolf, pp.6–7) becomes Walter Hardy, devotee of the gym. While the compassion shown by Hugh and Walter to their respective partners (Evelyn with an unknown internal disorder and HIV-positive Evan) finds favor with each Clarissa, the men are despised by other male characters—the spurned suitors. Peter Walsh regards Hugh as "nothing but manners" (Woolf, p.7); Richard Brown despises the confident muscularity of gay men like Walter, whose bodies bear no witness to the victimization they suffered as queer children.

Richard Brown, in being rejected as a life partner by Clarissa Vaughan, echoes Woolf's Peter Walsh. Both men belittle their respective Clarissas; "the perfect hostess" (Woolf, p.8), "a good suburban wife" (p.16). Cunningham's Clarissa is indeed as conventional as the original, although in the renewal of her narrative for the late twentieth century some of its aspects have been inverted. She too recalls a past kiss as a significant life moment but while Clarissa Dalloway's was boldly transgressive in being with another young woman, Sally Seton, Clarissa Vaughan's was with Richard Brown, a homosexual man. She too has suppressed the ambivalence of her sexuality: Clarissa Dalloway subdued her homo/sexual desire when choosing to marry Richard Dalloway while Clarissa Vaughan rejected a potentially heterosexual relationship with Richard Brown for life with a woman (Sally). During the day Sally finds her deep love for Clarissa invigorated, and she, like her template, Richard

Dalloway, buys roses as the only means of expressing this love. And while Sally is at a lunch to which Clarissa has not been invited, Clarissa Vaughan, like Clarissa Dalloway, is visited unexpectedly by a significant figure from the past. Louis Waters was Richard's lover when they were at Wellfleet. The three attempted a brief unhappy ménage-à-trois as Richard fell in love with Clarissa. In Cunningham's novel this site of adult memories of youthful possibilities (paralleling Bourton in *Mrs. Dalloway*) surely gains irony in being so geographically close to—but not—Provincetown, the Cape Cod town which welcomes gays and lesbians, and accommodates alternative arrangements. Louis is sore that Richard's book is devoted to Clarissa while he features only as a minor caricature. But like Peter Walsh, another oblique parallel, he arouses a sad envy in Clarissa when he claims to have fallen in love with a much younger partner. On hearing the news both Clarissas feel that that part of life—new lust—is over for them.

The relationship between *The Hours* and *Mrs. Dalloway* is impossible to simplify; Cunningham interweaves aspects of Woolf's life, her novel, and her theories. Like Woolf's Chinese boxes these narratives ceaselessly rotate within each other. Although the transposed story of *Mrs. Dalloway* is only one third of the triptych composing *The Hours*, the concerns of Woolf's novel—sex and love, sanity, madness, suicide, political power, the city—permeate beyond the explicit parallels detailed above, from and into the two other narratives. The character pairings not only occur between *Mrs. Dalloway* and the "Mrs. Dalloway" sections but across all three ("Mrs. Dalloway," "Mrs. Woolf," and "Mrs. Brown"). The formal and semantic similarities between the two novels as well as character duplication encourage and direct the reader to make these comparisons. For example, in writing a novel about the woman that he has re-christened Mrs. Dalloway, we are invited to read Richard Brown as doubling Virginia Woolf—herself a character in Cunningham's novel. Cunningham relates that in an early stage of writing *Mrs. Dalloway*, Woolf planned that her heroine would commit suicide. But in Cunningham's fiction, following an afternoon of quietly blissful contentment with her sister, nephews and niece, Woolf decides that Mrs. Dalloway—and by implication she herself at this moment—could not bear to leave all this: "There is so much in the world" (p.153). Cunningham thus presents a fictionalized Woolf as the original holder of this life-affirming philosophy—which is shared by both Clarissas—they assume to the scorn of Richard and Peter. But in Richard Brown's novel the character based around Clarissa Vaughan (whose name is not disclosed) apparently does die by her own hand. And Richard commits suicide like Woolf herself, although in the manner of one her characters. A familiarity with Woolf's novel thus generates germane questions about characters in *The Hours* such as: if Septimus Warren Smith's death enabled Clarissa Dalloway to live in *Mrs. Dalloway,* who lives on in Cunningham's novel upon the sacrificial embers of Richard Worthington Brown?

The answer can be deduced from a stylistic analysis of *Mrs. Dalloway* and *The Hours.* Cunningham has been praised for the ways his prose style emulates Woolf's without assuming parody. Woolf's presentation of multiple interior monologues, often the thoughts of characters who remain unprivileged and certainly extraneous to a "plot," has led *Mrs. Dalloway* to be defined as a novel about the fluidity of identity. Its decisive moment occurs, as we have seen, when Clarissa is externally viewed as singularly present and composed. At the end of the party and the novel, Peter Walsh, filled with an undefined excitement, seeks its source:

"It is Clarissa," he said.
   For there she was. (Woolf, p.255) [my italics]

The narrative is concluded as her competing identities have been temporally harmonized. *The Hours* meanwhile ends with the *self-definition* of Clarissa. Now that Richard has died there is no one to impose a name or, we infer, a narrative upon her.

> *And here she is,* herself, Clarissa, not Mrs. Dalloway anymore; there is no one now to call her that. (p.226) [my italics]

But in this novel of three narratives, the conclusion allows another major act of self-presentation. We have seen above that in *Mrs. Dalloway* Clarissa is externally defined through the narration of Peter Walsh. In *The Hours*, the Peter Walsh parallel figure, and definer, writer of fictions, Richard, is dead and so the narrative point of view is finally controlled by Clarissa herself. Unlike Richard and Peter Walsh, she strives to prevent herself from imposing definition upon Laura Brown, Richard's mother, who is the other figure achieving selfhood at the close of *The Hours*. Laura Brown is named in full for the first time:

> *Here she is,* then; the woman of wrath and sorrow, of pathos, of dazzling charm; the woman in love with death; the victim and torturer who haunted Richard's work. Here, right here in this room, is the beloved; the traitor. Here is an old woman, a retired librarian from Toronto, wearing old woman's shoes. (p. 226) [my italics]

Richard Brown's emotionally wrought perceptions of his mother, contained in his poetry, are here voiced by Clarissa — she only knows Laura through Richard's accounts and his verse — and then sympathetically deflated by her own physical description of the woman she sees before her. She is neither demon nor downtrodden, just an old woman in homely footwear. Laura is here, living and complete in the present, but it is only the death of her son, the writer, that has called her into *this* part of the text; *Clarissa's* narrative. Both women

are doubly fictioned—their thoughts shape their narrative components of Cunningham's novel, "Mrs. Dalloway," "Mrs. Brown"—
but in the story of *The Hours* they are also refashioned in Richard's
poetry and prose. These imaginary texts take on their own existence,
again ceaselessly rotating within Cunningham's story like Woolf's
Chinese boxes. In his enlargement of a novel about the narration of
identity, Cunningham is able to suggest a further consideration: the
extent to which identity is negotiated through narrative and fiction.

The female protagonists of the novels by Woolf and Cunningham
are drawn from very different social eras. That Clarissa Vaughan
lives in the time of greatest emancipation in Manhattan at the end of
the twentieth century is reflected in her self-definition and narrative
control at the end of *The Hours*. Progress in the empowerment of
women may be inferred from such a comparison of narrative point-
of-view in the definition of the novels' female protagonists. In 1920s'
London, Clarissa Dalloway is socially constructed through her married name and by a male suitor; in 1990s' New York, Clarissa
Vaughan eventually defines herself. In adopting Woolf's narrative
template, metaphors and motifs, Cunningham suggests however,
that social changes do not lead to significant differences in emotional experience.

The characters of both novels are in continual meditation upon
the success and failure of their lives, seeking external indicators of
worth and value in the material world in order to validate their judg-
ments. Virginia Woolf judges herself on the success of her novel,
Mrs. Brown on her cake, and Mrs. Dalloway on her party. In *Mrs.
Dalloway* these personal touchstones exist against a background of
publicly-esteemed people and patriarchal institutions, of parliament
and royalty. Cunningham updates this in *The Hours*: royalty's pow-
erful mystique has been replaced by the aura of majestic actresses.
Clarissa muses on the identity of a glimpsed movie star—is it Meryl
Streep or perhaps Vanessa Redgrave? Cunningham seems playful

here: in 1997 Vanessa Redgrave performed the title role in the screen adaptation of *Mrs. Dalloway* (dir. Marleen Gorris). But the reader of Cunningham's novel is afforded a further level of intertextuality, as Meryl Streep plays Clarissa Vaughan in the film version of *The Hours*.

Within *The Hours* Richard's novel has not achieved the market recognition that would lead to a film adaptation—"It was curtly reviewed" (p.16)—but has received some critical approbation. His version of Clarissa's life has been externally validated through the award of the Carrouthers Prize: only granted when a work is deemed incontrovertibly outstanding. But Richard finds no affirmation of value in the prize feeling instead that he has been awarded a public recognition of his illness. In *Mrs. Dalloway* it was the absence of understanding of the damages of war that drove Septimus Warren Smith to suicide; he was encouraged to repress his memories. But for Richard, his double, whose artistic expression has been fostered and "eagerly-anticipated" (p.16), the urge of the community ravaged by AIDS to embrace his suffering feels like another way of negating his art: "I got a prize for having AIDS and going nuts and being brave about it, it had nothing to do with my work" (p.63). Cunningham continues Woolf's metaphorical representation of the flux of despair through watery metaphors of sinking, plunging, rising, and surface, images made all the more potent by her own drowning.

In these meditations upon methods of determining value both novels subject art and lives to the same scrutiny (unsurprisingly in texts which ultimately pronounce the indivisibility of all forms of narrative). In *The Hours* the final criterion of judgment is time. Time in all its forms—anticipated or recalled, clock-measured, or replayed through memory—is a structural device in Woolf's novel, which takes place over one waking day, after all. Time and narrative will be discussed below, but here it should be observed that Cunningham's engagement with time, like Woolf's, goes beyond the organizational. In his novel of mortal illness and suicides time has become all; one can exult "only in continuance" (p.29). The hours then, are those that remain to be lived. Richard cannot face his hours, as, due to his mental debilitation, his contain neither memories nor the refashioning of old stories or the conjuring of new ones. Survival equals success in this novel, not because longevity is valued in itself, but because remaining hours, like new lovers, are a future with narrative possibilities, they may contain moments of "everything we've ever imagined" (p. 225).

"The Hours" and The Hours: *narrative and time*

As Woolf developed her short story "Mrs. Dalloway in Bond Street" into a novel, she provisionally called it "The Hours," before returning to an abbreviation of the original, *Mrs. Dalloway.* "The Hours" suggests a significant preoccupation with demarcations and narrative depictions of time; Woolf's prose has always lent itself to interpretation through temporal analysis. Readings commonly posit a Bergsonian rejection of clock time for the more "real" emotional time implied in the title of her memoir *Moments of Being*—and this is tacitly supported by her dismissal of "The Hours" (clock time) for the momentary coherent identity suggested in the name *Mrs. Dalloway.* That Woolf's characters are commonly presented as experiencing "moments of being" analeptically, through memory, anticipates a Derridean understanding that individuated moments—uninscribed by the past or the future—are as elusive as undivided identity. Both can only be expressed as desires. When *Mrs. Dalloway* climaxes with a moment of selfhood, it is a moment perceived through the focalization of another character; it is the desire of Peter Walsh.

Derrida and deconstructive critics called into question the concept of linear time—and the positivism of cause and effect. They sought to replace the progression of past, present and future, with the idea of the "trace" in which every component of a sequence — linguistic or narrative — is understood to impact upon the others. A word's meaning, for instance, cannot be understood in isolation from its context, its sentence, its text. Each word bears the traces of those that surround and have surrounded it. A text cannot be understood outside its discourse of other texts. Derrida described the traces as "ever-receding" back to a posited long-forgotten original. It is not simply in transposing *Mrs. Dalloway* that Cunningham's novel points to this cultural concern with and mythologizing of origin and originality. In sharing Woolf's working title, *The Hours* itself is a subtle disruption of linear chronology: it positions itself as preceding her published novel. Analyzing the postmodern trend of spectrality in contemporary art — as opposed to an earlier modernist anxiety or ecstasy of influence — Hal Foster suggests that the "shadowing in play today is more muted, a sort of outlining and shading, in the manner that *Mrs. Dalloway* (1925) outlines and shades *The Hours* (1998) by Michael Cunningham" (Hal Foster, *Design and Crime*, p.134). Despite the careful ambivalence of the term "shadow" — a shadow can fall in front of or behind an object, it depends where you stand — Foster fails to consider the fact that once you have read *The Hours* you cannot replace *Mrs. Dalloway* outside *its* sphere of influence. Foster is right to accept Derrida's notion of hauntology as the dominant influence on discourse today, however, his semantic positioning of *Mrs. Dalloway* as shadowing *The Hours* fails on several levels to consider the existence of both novels as textual narratives (Foster's polemic is mainly concerned with architecture and the visual arts). I think he underestimates the degree of explicit engagement of Cunningham's novel with Woolf's and the way *The Hours* now haunts *Mrs. Dalloway* and not vice versa. Cunningham's novel may send readers back and to *Mrs. Dalloway* but now through her existence as a fictional character within his book, we are directed to find her in specific features of her own (which I shall discuss below).

Even from the title then, we understand that *The Hours* cannot simply be a rewriting of *Mrs. Dalloway* for it disrupts the notion of an original and an influenced text. Linear sequence is also disturbed within the novel—not just in the title—through engagement with the refutation of authorial intention: the death of the author. Barthes's memorable epithet is a warning against reading for a single privileged meaning, one that stems from an idea of a fixed identity of one individual (the author). If we were to depict reading for authorial intent as a linear sequence of cause and effect, it would look like this: author → text → reader. This directional order authorizes against intertextuality and the trace, in recognizing one isolated source of the text. It underplays the vulnerability of the text to readers' varied interpretations and instead relies upon a construction of the author as conscious of and in control of his meanings. As we have seen Cunningham includes two authorial figures in *The Hours*. By inserting Virginia Woolf into the "Mrs. Woolf" sections of the novel as a character writing "The Hours" he proposes a symptomatic reading of *Mrs. Dalloway* which exposes a mechanical relationship between her biography and her fiction. But the idea of authority through narration—which Cunningham presents Woolf as seeking and which was temporally resolved at the close of *Mrs. Dalloway*, as described above—implodes in Cunningham's novel in his other author character, Richard Brown. Richard's deconstructive agency stems from both his position as author and from the narrative representation of his confusion. It is his position as author of the unnamed novel within the story that causes the crux that prevents a reading of even the "Mrs. Dalloway" sections of *The Hours* as a simple updating of *Mrs. Dalloway*. The novel's most significant temporal disjunctions and narrative gaps occur within the chapters he inhabits. They raise questions about *The Hours* that remain logically unanswerable and point instead to the authorial figure's fluid and indeterminate identity, and thus an inability to point to one privileged source of a narrative. We cannot tell where his fictions begin or end.

The "Mrs. Dalloway" sections of *The Hours* are narrated from Clarissa's point of view. It is the day that Richard will be awarded the Carrouthers Prize for his novel. However, when Clarissa first visits him he starts to "remember" attending the ceremony and the celebration even though they have yet to take place. He asks to see the trophy that he has yet to be awarded. Initially aware that these things are both in the future and yet can be recollected, he explains "I seem to have fallen out of time" (p.62). With the substitution of one verb the phrase jars in its approximation to "running out of time" and in its anticipation of his suicide in which he both "falls out" of the window and "runs out" of time. His ravaged mind has rendered him temporally and linguistically confused; time seems to be a physical space.

In fact, for the dying man time is becoming a merely physical experience. While his "muscles and organs have been revived" (p.56) by new drugs his mind is a chaos of voices startled by moments of lucidity. Some of the voices even appear to be Woolf's; he speaks some of her suicide note before he dies. Aware that his body endures while his mind deteriorates, Richard is afraid because soon meaningless time, blank hours, will be all he has: "One and then another, and you get through that one and then, my god, there's another" (pp.197–8). He has no future: as his mind disintegrates, his existence can only be corporeal—he will become simply an object. Frederic Jameson has described the fragmentary character of postmodernity as schizophrenic: the schizophrenic is condemned to live a perpetual present because s/he cannot recognize the past and future in language articulation. Richard cannot separate the past, present and future, nor distinguish temporal or physical space in language. Soon as no more than a breathing body, incapable of coherent thought and expression, he will only exist in a continuous present. His bold recognition that he only has "the hours" left prompts his suicide: he can no longer author a single coherent narrative. He expresses the condition of postmodernity.

There are moments in the story when Richard appears to be already living a perpetual present. His love affair with Clarissa has shaped both their lives. He talks to her of a poignant moment:

> "You kissed me beside a pond."
> "Ten thousand years ago."
> "It's still happening."
> "In a sense, yes."
> "In reality. It's happening in that present. This is happening in this present." (p.66)

Clarissa attributes Richard's confusion of time and space to his tiredness and medication, however, his disorientation raises questions about the demarcations of narrative for us as readers. The continuous separate presents he imagines—"that present . . . this present" (p.66)—may be the different narratives of his life; the one he lived, the one he had hoped for, the novel he wrote about Clarissa, and *Mrs. Dalloway*, the novel he imagined her living. But it is impossible for the reader to try and unravel the differences and segregate these narratives—if we try our confusion begins to resemble his. As readers of *The Hours* we know that the story in some way resembles that of Woolf's novel. As I have outlined above many events and characters are shared. However, this seems to be both known and unknown within the story; Clarissa is tired of Richard calling her Mrs. Dalloway and yet seems remarkably unaware of the fictional pattern of events that she follows. Although the focalization of the "Mrs. Dalloway" chapters is apparently hers she makes no wry comment upon the fact that like her fictional counterpart she's holding a party and she bought the flowers for it herself. Could the narrative point of view thus be someone else's? Are we in fact reading Richard's—conspicuously untitled—novel about Clarissa? What are the alternative rational explanations for her failure to recognize the pattern within the story? But if it is his novel and focalization, his updating of *Mrs. Dalloway*, which we read within the "Mrs. Dalloway" sections then how can it continue after his death? This is the unresolved disruption of the linear sequence of author → novel → reader → influenced novel, in *The Hours*. Richard's novel both is and isn't "Mrs. Dalloway." This crux highlights the indivisibility of lives and fictions and belies the simplicity with which we accept Cunningham's symptomatic, biographically-informed reading of Woolf's intention for *Mrs. Dalloway* in his "Mrs. Woolf" chapters. Richard's death is an event within the story, but as "the death of the author" is also a rhetorical gesture.

There is a great deal of pathos in Richard's plight, his sense of failure and the dissolution of his authorial identity. Richard's suicide speaks of his sense of redundancy as an artist. He fears that not only is he becoming objectified through the loss of his mind, but that it is his sick body that is being honored in the Carrouthers Prize rather than his fiction, as we have seen. He has attempted to preserve the "lost" narratives of his life with Clarissa but even she too expresses the fear that his novel belongs to the "world of objects" (p.22) and not endlessly renewable narratives. Objects are symptomatic of clock time in *The Hours*. When Clarissa considers alternative lives that she might have chosen—"her other home, where neither Sally nor Richard exists; where there is only the essence of Clarissa, a girl grown into a woman, still full of hope, still capable of anything" (p.92)—it is the materiality of her apartment and its contents that she must abandon to enable her to be the person her youthful self had envisaged. Her anxiety that books can provide no comfort because they belong to the "world of objects" is a concern that art is in fact synchronic, that like furniture and ornaments which date and decay, books are finite, rigid markers of clock time, unlike the endless renewability of narratives and the infinity of meanings they inspire.

Unsurprisingly perhaps, given their explicit reference to the earlier novel, the "Mrs. Dalloway" sections of *The Hours* engage more expressly with ideas about narrative than the two other stories in the triptych. It is another contemporary critical truism that to be human is to create stories; within *The Hours* narratives are created, and offered, as generous acts. But—as though Woolf had never written— Clarissa fears that published fiction cannot compare to personal narratives, memories. She wants to give HIV-positive Evan "the book of his own life, the book that will locate him, parent him" (p.22) but pessimistically doubts that any book can convey what her earliest memory holds for her. Richard's fear of "the hours" is a fear of experiencing only clock time; he will no longer be able to defy linear time with narratives of the past and the future. Clarissa's optimism about Richard's work entering the canon, being fired into the future, seems as misjudged as the rockets on Richard's childish robe that the phrase calls to mind. Richard commits suicide: he doesn't fear his own death—the death of the author—but fears instead, the privileging of the author—his body—over his body of work.

"Mrs. Woolf:" the death of the author

Richard Brown is the second author imagined in Cunningham's novel. Some readings of *The Hours* as "docu-novel" (Joyce Carol Oates, Salon.Com, 20 September 1999) overlook that Woolf is a fictional character within it. In the prologue Cunningham tenderly recreates the final moments of her life. The intense observations of nature which characterized her prose are emulated and gain further poignancy in being the last impressions she absorbs before death: "she can't help noticing the stone's cold chalkiness and its color, a milky brown with spots of green" (p.4). The weight of the stone in her pocket allows her to be dragged under the water; as its current bears her body away the narrative presents her body as still receiving images: of shafts of light in the water, tangled weed, clouds above the surface. It is almost as though her artistry is corporeal—her body of work is figured on her dead body as it is swept away. Carried by the river's current she seems to embody the term that is readily (mis) applied to her prose style; the "stream-of-consciousness" flows on. Meanwhile Leonard reads the real suicide note that Woolf left him. It is a bold and haunting introduction to *The Hours*, an amalgamation of poetic license and documentary evidence. Cunningham has attended closely to the content and style of Woolf's diaries and letters, and to biographies: it is perhaps this beguiling proximity that has upset some of Woolf's admirers, for the account of Woolf does contain fabrication and deviations from the chronology and substance of her life.

Cunningham himself has suggested that opening with Woolf's self-annihilation was almost unavoidable. He claims to have acknowledged it in order to "dispatch it" because we are transfixed by the knowledge that she—like Sylvia Plath—killed herself. But of course, the prologue has the opposite effect; just as thoughts of her suicide inform our readings of her life and fiction, it casts a shadow over the rest of *The Hours*, making us fearful of the fragility and despair of many of the characters, especially Laura and Richard Brown. It decides the tone of the novel and is thematically crucial. Right from the start it ignites the theoretical concern of the "death of the author" as discussed above—Woolf dies in the prologue to a novel in which she appears as a character writing a novel. Although there is a biographical explanation for her death, as with Richard

Brown her death as surrogate authorial figure is an assimilation of a critical debate into the novel. Her centrality to *The Hours* as character and, it could be argued, author of some of it ("Mrs. Dalloway") creates an irony in that Cunningham's own authorial agency becomes somewhat erased. In this representation of authorial figures it is easy to forget Cunningham's artistry: whereas the gaps between biographical accounts of Woolf's life and his narrative disclose a symptomatic reading of his project.

The "Mrs. Woolf" component of the triptych condenses factual elements from Woolf's life during the two years in which she wrote *Mrs. Dalloway* into one imaginary day in which she begins to write the novel. Woolf herself engaged in biographical fictions—*Orlando* (1928) is a poetic fantasy based around the life of her friend Vita Sackville-West. And she wrote many essays defining the New Biography as an art in lively contrast to the monumentalization and memorialism of Victorian epic lives and biographies. Cunningham's style, however, does not seek to dramatize the conflict between fact and fiction as hers did (Laura Marcus, *Auto/Biographical Discourses*, pp.116–27). His style is more sedate, thus leading to the concerns that *his* Virginia Woolf is not recognized as a fiction but—despite its entrance into interior realms, its poetic trajectory through her dying moments—as somehow a verbatim account of a period of her life. There is a further unintended irony in Cunningham's foregrounding of Woolf's dead body in his novel, for she argued against the thanatography of Victorian biographers, their morbid memorializing of their subjects' corpses.

Cunningham's narrative, the focalization of Woolf's meditations as she wrote, is a convincing marriage of the domestic concerns on a writing day, how they become woven into her fiction, and the ensuing oscillations between confidence and despair about her writing and her sanity. Hermione Lee, Woolf's acclaimed biographer and admirer of *The Hours*, has found Cunningham's "tiny deviations

from fact" *(Times Literary Supplement* 1.8.99, http://www.the-tls
.co.uk) irksome, perhaps because of their subtlety. For example, the
day that Cunningham creates (in June 1923) is not the day that she
dies but because of its proleptic presentation we read the anxieties
of the day—from encroaching madness to her lack of authority over
Nelly, the cook—as generating the despair that led to her self-annihilation some eighteen years later in 1941.

I will suggest later that Cunningham's condensation of events is
an over-determined reading of Woolf's life. It serves the emotional
truth of her character as he perceives it as well as the narrative sus-
pense of his fiction. Lee has pointed out that the "perilous night
when Virginia nearly rushed off to London on the train, but was
stopped by meeting Leonard, was in Sussex, not Richmond, and in
September, not June." (ibid.). Fearing a decline into insanity, "the
nearness of the old devil" (p.167) she goes for a walk and decides to
confront and thus hopefully assuage her madness by taking a train
to the capital to roam its streets. It is a barely reassuring moment in
the fictional June day when Leonard does rescue his wife, for we
have already read—in the prologue—of the moment when he did
not. At the time of writing "The Hours" the couple lived in Richmond, a quieter environment than London's metropolitan chaos
and social scene, and one that Leonard thought conducive to her
sanity. But Woolf longed to return to the capital and what Cunningham has convincingly summarized as "all that London implies
about freedom, about kisses, about the possibilities of art and the sly
dark glitter of madness" (p.172). The fictional day closes with joy
when a return to London is agreed, a fictionalization of a biographical event. It was Woolf's enthusiasm for the city upon her return that
inspired its celebration in *Mrs. Dalloway.*

Cunningham's portrayal of Woolf is generous and deeply sympathetic. Through his fictionalized biography he bestows a humanity

upon her, one that is not always perceived by those who criticize her fiction and the perceived elitism and political apathy of the Bloomsbury set. Her snobbishness and preoccupation with her lack of authority over her servants become in Cunningham's representation a symptom of the fragility of her own sense of self, and perhaps the denial of maternity enforced upon her. It is widely held that Woolf was deterred from becoming a mother by her doctors, and by Leonard acting upon their advice. Cunningham emphasizes this reading in his repeated use of maternity as a metaphor and in another transgression from the chronology of Woolf's life. Ralph Partridge had already left the Hogarth Press (the Woolf's publishing house) when she wrote *Mrs. Dalloway* but in *The Hours*, his existence facilitates a moment in which Woolf considers her relationship with him through remembrance of her own mother.

In his most elaborate freedom with biography Cunningham affords Woolf an illicit moment of victory when she kisses her sister Vanessa. Although innocent it "feels like the most delicious and forbidden of pleasures" (p.154) for it takes place secretly, in the kitchen, Nelly's domain, and behind her back. Cunningham makes Woolf fearful of Nelly and aware of her own ineptitude as a mistress—her own desire to redress this in her fiction (through Mrs. Dalloway's favorable relationships with her servants) is smiled upon as human weakness in his. However, Cunningham's representation of Woolf's creative genius does not suggest a banal fixation with social inadequacy as her motivation for writing, it is rather a compulsion that at best emanates from an unconscious "inner faculty that recognizes the animating mysteries of the world because it is made of the same substance" (p.35). She writes through dreams—rather than language—and always against a relapse into insanity. Cunningham's poetic depiction of her creative process precariously balanced upon a surface that may collapse into vacuums of despair employs a narrative and metaphorical style that aligns her—as his fictional character—with one of her own fictional creations. In *The Hours*, through the representation of her as author, she becomes a Woolfian character—it is a further validation of her narrative style, and his, that she is humanized through Cunningham's adoption of her style.

Mrs. Brown: all about my mothers

One of these days Mrs. Brown will be caught.
(Woolf, *Essays Volume* 3, p.388)

In summer 1923 as Woolf wrote "The Hours," reviews of her previous novel, *Jacob's Room* (1922), were being published. Their criticisms preoccupied her; she was particularly exercised by the novelist Arnold Bennett's critique of her characterization. In her considered response, published first as an essay—"Mr. Bennett and Mrs. Brown"—and then expanded into a paper given at Cambridge the following year—"Character in Fiction"—she asserted that since "All human relations have shifted" (Woolf, *Essays Volume* 3, p. 422) her contemporaries must forge a new style of writing rather than look to traditional novels as models. Life had changed—famously in or around 1910, the year of the first exhibition of Post-Impressionist painting in Britain—and now prose fiction must adapt to record it. In particular—and anticipating Barthes—the elevation of the author must cease and a new democracy between author and reader must be established. The living novelist faced the greatest challenge of literary history: to shape a spirited figure from the ruins of the Victorians' vivid metonyms and the Russians' excavations deep into the psyche. Thus far, Woolf claimed, this being had eluded capture on the page. But when she was caught—and Woolf uses the female pronoun—when novels spoke of domesticity as well as war, English literature itself would be transformed. The name she gave this elusive character of modern fiction was Mrs. Brown.

In "Character in Fiction" Woolf elaborates upon the life of this depleted old woman, whose name bespeaks an ordinariness, as an advocation of presenting life "as it is" and not "how it should be" (for which she chides Arnold). For Mrs. Brown with her "clean little boots" (Woolf, *Essays Volume* 3, p.423), like Cunningham's Laura Brown with her "old woman's shoes" (p.226), shares the qualities of fragility and heroism. In embodying the theories of "Character in Fiction" Cunningham updates this "homely" example in Laura Brown. Ironically he also found Mrs. Brown evasive, even though— or perhaps because—he has referred to her as his mother (Canning, N. pag.). For Cunningham, the character of Laura only rose above stereotype—of the unhappy 1950s' housewife—when he chose to think of her as an artist. He has spoken of a parallel between Woolf's desire to write a great novel and Laura's yearnings to create the perfect home. In calling her "Mrs. Brown" Cunningham alludes to the creation of literary character (Woolf's essay) while narrating an experience of maternity.

The theme of motherhood resounds throughout Cunningham's novels, but finds its central construct in *The Hours* in pregnant Laura Brown, whose misery stems from the conflicts of being a mother. Laura fears that she cannot discover her true talents while devoting herself to her son; the life she has imagined, her character, has escaped. Like Clarissas Vaughan and Dalloway, Laura is tormented by the perception that others slight her, her marriage especially. Her husband, Dan, a World War II veteran who was believed to have died in Japan, "could (in the words of his own alarmed mother) have had anyone" but instead chose her "the bookworm, the foreign-looking one" (p.40). Laura struggles to make the ordered and harmonious home a war hero deserves; she is taut between her ravenous love for her small son, Richie; her secret desire to be brilliant and create a perfect home, and a profound despondency. She reads to escape from this anxiety.

But what is the connection between Woolf's literary theories and the theme of maternity in *The Hours?* Cunningham does not present Woolf as understanding her creativity through the tired but enduring trope of childbirth, nor does he capitalize on her role as a "literary mother," providing the role model she found so lacking in Arnold, and that she explored in her polemical *A Room of One's Own* (1929). Instead, as we have seen, Cunningham figures Woolf's anxieties about not being a mother through metaphor. Throughout the novel motherhood is synonymous with an inscrutable competence: Cunningham's narrators often describe capability as mother "like." For instance, Woolf decides that Clarissa Dalloway will command respect from her servants by speaking to them in a tone that is "motherly but not familiar" (p.87). She perceives her sister, Vanessa Bell, as having inherited the maternal confidence of their own mother, and as such she becomes a source of anxiety. Woolf finds Vanessa's competence "impenetrable," mysterious and threatening in the way it points to a lack in herself. Having children "is the true accomplishment; this will live after the tinselly experiments in narrative" which will become outmoded (p.118). In making Woolf voice this fear Cunningham implies that Arnold's criticism of her characters as insubstantial and transient was not just a critique of her fiction, but threatened her entire sense of purpose and self-identity. Unlike Vanessa's children, Woolf fears her creations, her books, would not survive. As we have seen continuance is valued in *The Hours*, however, Cunningham counters Woolf's despondency through the figure of Laura Brown whose endurance — she outlives her husband and her children — is enabled by the refuge she finds in reading Woolf's prose, *Mrs. Dalloway.*

Laura Brown's flight from her life as mother and wife echoes Clarissa Dalloway's withdrawal from the marital bed, humorously signaled in her preferred bed-time reading: historical memoirs which detail the "retreat from Moscow" (Woolf, p.40). Both heroines lose themselves in prose but unlike Clarissa, Laura cannot escape from her husband's bed to a single bed in the attic. Instead she leaves her son with a neighbor and guiltily, as though she is having an affair, books into a hotel; a foretaste, we later learn, of leaving her family for good. When she finds peace in a hotel room she imagines that death would be as appealing. In this chapter Cunningham reproduces some passages from *Mrs. Dalloway*—not only to point out parallels for readers unfamiliar with Woolf's novel—but to engender a shared experience or identification with his protagonist. We read what Laura reads.

This submersion directly into Laura's experience through reading the modernist text allows for a further interpretation of the novel through psychoanalytical theories of language and maternity; it is almost an enactment of Kristevan semiotic theory. When Woolf's novels were reclaimed by feminist scholars of the late 1970s and 1980s, the theories of French philosopher Julia Kristeva were popularly applied as an explanation of their narrative fluidity. Kristeva challenged the notion of a fixed coherent ego, claiming instead that the "symbolic self" was a momentary position in language (the symbolic order) continually threatened by semiotic impulses. As a state of pre-linguistic fluctuation, governed by drives and rooted in infancy, the semiotic may be broadly characterized as maternal as opposed to the paternal law of the symbolic order. It is rhythmic and musical as opposed to rational and linear; the non-verbal "singing" of the old woman by the tube station in *Mrs. Dalloway* has for instance been cited as an example of a semiotic drive to disrupt language. Laura is lulled into a semiotic state by Woolf's incantory prose. Kristeva's adaptation of Lacan's psychoanalytical theories is useful for a reading of *The Hours* in clearly highlighting a relationship between two predominant concerns of the novel: maternity and language. Laura is distressed by her role within the symbolic order (wife and mother) and so escapes it by immersion into the flux of Woolf's prose.

Is Laura's flight from maternity ever resolved? Did she remain forever lost to Richard—Richie—the son whose writings sought to find her? How successful were his attempts to capture Mrs. Brown? The answers to these questions remain to some extent within *The Hours*: Richard is dead, *his* poems are not reproduced, and we have only access to Clarissa's musings at the conclusion of the novel. Clarissa's doubts about her own success as a mother, however, seem at least momentarily resolved, when Julia handles the aftermath of the cancelled party with assurance. Clarissa's status as a mother is as threatening to the symbolic order as Laura's is threatened by it, for she has procreated without a man. Her anxieties about being a bad mother are in fact about paternal absence; having conceived her daughter through anonymous artificial insemination she feels sure that her daughter hates her for denying her a father. With a streak of jealous cruelty she tells herself that her daughter's friendship with bull dyke Mary Krull is an attempt to find a father figure—in turn a reference to readings of *Mrs. Dalloway* which find Elizabeth replacing her mother with a sanctimonious and unattractive woman, Miss Kilman.

The composure and maturity of Julia at the close of *The Hours* may serve as counterbalance to readings of the unhappy relationship between Richard and his mother as a demonstration of the theories of psychoanalysts such as Irving Bieber (discussed above) who found that homosexuality was the result of severe emotional problems in their parents. The dyad of weak father and strong mother is revisited throughout Cunningham's novels to the extent that fathers in *The Hours* are utterly marginalized by the text, while motherhood is figured almost as much through absence as presence. In the "Mrs. Brown" chapters for example, the childlessness of Laura's married neighbor Kitty is a source of speculation to her community, forever hanging like an invisible question mark above her head. Their kiss is a rare but troubling moment of pleasure outside of books for Laura. She recognizes and is fearful of the agency of her transgression; as Bergman points out homophobic attitudes were far stronger in the 1950s than the 1920s and '30s. Laura—resident of the conservative suburbs, a mother who seeks perfection, a repressed lesbian, apparently the cause of her son's unhappiness and "dysfunction"—stands at the center of the triptych. Her pathos and the poignancy with which it is drawn oppose an imposition of Bieber's etiology upon the novel; Cunningham defies us to read her as "guilty" of her son's unhappiness.

Cities

It is significant that the closing moments of coherent selfhood for both Clarissa Dalloway and Clarissa Vaughan take place within their own homes. Until then their meandering meditations upon life and identity are shaped by their perambulations as they encounter friends, the famous, and vagrants on the streets of Westminster and the West Village respectively. Both protagonists are flâneurs; they walk through the cities in order to live, joyously receiving impressions of public life through encounters, overheard conversations and the histories embodied in the buildings and monuments of cities. The street scenes of both novels are vibrant; celebrations of London and New York themselves and the freedoms and opportunities offered to those who are able to walk in them. In *Mrs. Dalloway* and *The Hours* cities are metonymies of social life, contrasting with the unhappiness of the isolated or constrained self, such as the insanity of Septimus Warren Smith, Woolf and Richard Brown, and Laura's stifling domesticity.

Clarissa Dalloway is able later to attain momentary selfhood precisely because she has been able to wander freely, undifferentiated from the world, merging through overheard fragments of conversation and even being recalled back down the years to prehistory by the wordless song of an old flower-seller. Clarissa Vaughan's narrative also begins with her absorption into her neighborhood. She too celebrates the city's indestructability doubting its existence in any other form even though she knows "the story about Manhattan as a wilderness purchased for strings of beads" (p.14). She contrasts her "indiscriminate love" for its every feature, ugly or squalid, with Richard's view; he would "edit the morning" in his narrative (p.12). Her embracing of every feature, her willingness to be absorbed by the streets, is also contrasted with the muscularity of Walter Hardy whose vulnerability has been defied through the fiercely honed armor of his body. His corporeality denies fusion—just as his romantic novels deny narrative uncertainty—while Clarissa's corporeal existence is almost erased from her narrative in favor of the impressions she receives of her environment. Kristevan readings defend this submission to the semiotic, women's right "to merge" (Jean Wyatt, "Avoiding Self-Definition: In Defense of Women's Right to Merge: Julia Kristeva and *Mrs. Dalloway*").

Instead, Clarissa Vaughan becomes a conduit; her short walk transmits a picture of the West Village in the late twentieth century, seemingly in sharp contrast to the locality of her literary namesake. At first Clarissa Dalloway's London, represented by Westminster and the luxurious shops of Bond Street in the West End, seems the site of wealth, power and authority. Home to parliament and Big Ben, the penetrating symbol of public order, its monuments to conquest and empire loom large. Their colonization of the streets is disrupted however, by those who cannot be regimented, the thoughts of passers by, voices of the insane and non-verbal euphoria of the homeless and dispossessed. In name, Clarissa Vaughan's West Village echoes the Westminster of *Mrs. Dalloway* with a further echo of Greenwich Mean Time, located in London, and in Greenwich Village. In the

1960s this area of Manhattan as a site of dissidence (the site of the Stonewall riots) *was* a precise inversion of Westminster, but by the 1990s of *The Hours* it is home to a new kind of establishment. Clarissa Vaughan and Sally are members of the media cognoscenti rather more influential and wealthy than the artists and political dissidents on whose nonconformism the area still trades. Clarissa enjoys a momentary, almost Woolfian, snobbishness as she considers that "the neighborhood today is an imitation of itself, a watered-down carnival" selling cheap ephemera for tourists (p.52). Even so the fakery of these coffee shops is disturbed by the billowing litter, furniture abandoned on the sidewalks, and most of all again the narratives of those who still populate the streets. As in Woolf's Westminster they are a place to encounter stories of private lives and personal tragedies. We hear of the temporary abeyance of Evan's declining t-cell count in a meeting with his partner, and learn that Barbara, the flower shop owner, has failed in her career as an opera singer but has escaped breast cancer.

In opening *The Hours* with this affirmation of the flâneur, of the possibilities alive to those who can roam freely, a clear sense of all that the Virginia Woolf character yearns for as a social being and a writer is established. The narrative journey of *The Hours* is not single—Clarissa's small voyage to self-identity—but interwoven. Because we have witnessed Woolf's final journey in Cunningham's text, then Clarissa's joyous perambulations, a deep sympathy is engendered for Woolf's plight, trapped in the isolating, unstimulating suburbs. A phrase from *Mrs. Dalloway* which unites the city with life at its fullest—"life, London, this moment in June" (p.111)—is repeated in Laura Brown's narrative becoming almost a touchstone in moments of happiness. The thought of Woolf's London and all the freedoms it represents becomes a life force for Mrs. Brown. She recalls it significantly after the exhilaration of her kiss with Kitty when life seems suddenly open to possibilities once more. Cunningham's novel amplifies the sense in *Mrs. Dalloway* of the streets as not simply an archive of personal stories, prehistoric and civic histories, but the location of fertility of the future. When Clarissa Vaughan envies Louis's new love affair—as Clarissa Dalloway is quietly discontented by Peter Walsh's forthcoming nuptials—her distress is phrased in an echo of the Woolf character's yearning for the "sly dark glitter" of the metropolis (p.172); she wants to be released to experience the anguish and exhilaration of the streets. For them the city is a place of sexual possibility—even if possibility rather than enactment is all that is desired. In the novel's closest moment to (desired) sexual intercourse, Sally, full of love for Clarissa, saunters home through the streets with her roses, hopeful for a physical celebration of their union "How long has it been since they've had sex?" (p.185).

Those who survive in *The Hours* are those who are exposed to and submit to narratives other than their own, through city streets or through reading. Both enable a dissolution of selfhood that *The Hours*, like *Mrs. Dalloway*, validates as a necessity of survival.

A democracy of despondency: narrative, creativity and despair

In her study of the pervasive cultural association of women and madness, Elaine Showalter reflects on the construction of the creative madwoman as an emblematic figure for feminist literary historians: "Biographies and letters of gifted women who suffered mental breakdowns have suggested that madness is the price women artists have had to pay for the exercise of their creativity in a male-dominated culture" (Elaine Showalter, *The Female Malady*, p.4). Such biographical readings have led to a reification of the insanity of authors like Woolf, Anne Stevenson and Sylvia Plath, leading to single-faceted (and defiantly feminist) symptomatic readings of their fiction. While Hermione Lee provides a sensitive account of the treatments Woolf underwent for her neurasthenia and recognizes the way her mental fragility may have shaped her narrative style, she seeks to redress such narrow interpretations of Woolf's fiction as being colonized by madness, and her whole life as falling in the shadow of suicide. She "fought to put her illness to good use" (Lee, p.456) and while her writing was "wrestled from illness, fear and pain," "hers was a life of heroism not oppression" (Lee, p.199).

Although Cunningham's biographical fiction is informed by Lee's biography—as he tells us in his Note on Sources—it is very much an account of the interdependency of Woolf's creativity and fear of insanity. As Lee proposes, the theme of heroism is dominant, present in all three components of his triptych. The novel ends after all on a triumphant note for the character of Woolf, not chronologically with her suicide but as she is about to return to the social life of London. Unlike in *Mrs. Dalloway* there are no merciless doctors in *The Hours*; the novel is a deeply sympathetic account of those whose lives are plagued by the fear of encroaching madness, oscillating between control and numb despair, and the people who try their best to care for them.

Cunningham offers three characters whose lives are tormented by the pursuit of perfection in their art: Virginia Woolf, Richard Brown and Laura Brown. We understand the pressures upon each character fully through recognition of the triptych as a whole rather than through discrete consideration of each; Woolf's biography and presentations of madness within her fiction gives agency to their despair. Laura's domestic frustration echoes the tedium of life in suburban Richmond for Woolf. Like Woolf and Laura, Richard is defeated by creative failings; like Woolf's character, Septimus Warren Smith, he is rendered incoherent by destructive treatment for an illness endemic to his society—for Septimus shell-shock, for Richard, AIDS. Cunningham does not resolve the intractable question of the causal relationship between society, insanity and artistic excellence and innovation—his is not a novel of simply posited demarcations after all—but instead recognizes a democracy of despondency, one which echoes the democracy of Woolf's prose, the narrative generosity which allows all to speak their interiorized anxieties. We feel Laura's bleakness and understand her frustration about her cake as much as we fear Woolf's submission to non-being.

Cunningham's repetition of metaphors, thematic and semantic structures underlines the commonality of experience between the characters. Laura Brown's day echoes Virginia Woolf's; both spend the morning engrossed in creative acts; both feel a female visitor exposes their lack of conventional femininity; and in the afternoon both take temporary flight from home. Cunningham elevates Laura's cake baking to artistic production, through expression of her anxiety for its perfection and paralleling these emotions with Woolf. The Woolf character expresses the gap between the "better book in one's mind than one can manage to get onto paper" (p.69) while later Mrs. Brown's cake does not turn out "the way she'd pictured it" (p.99). The portentous influence of the Woolf chapters— essentially as prologued by her suicide—upon the narrative depiction of Laura creates a tension that leads us to suppose that she too will take her own life. However, within the present of the text it is Richard who reaches the bitter end of this cruel trajectory. He has already descended into the annihilating incoherence that Woolf fears. His novel has already failed. He has acceded to Woolf's insanity: he speaks with her voice—from her suicide note—and is tormented by the Greek voices that famously characterized her bouts of madness.

In her analysis of Woolf's letters and diaries Lee notes that she often used the same words to describe literary pressures and the treatment of her madness, feeling coerced into both. Cunningham emphasizes this symbiosis of writing and insanity in his depiction of

Woolf; her meditations upon intelligibility develop from reflections upon the difficulties of writing into fears for her sanity—"if she pushes beyond her limits she will taint the whole enterprise. She will let it wander into a realm of incoherence from which it might never return" (p.70). Within *The Hours* it is Richard who succumbs to the annihilating solipsism that characterizes Woolf's fictional depictions of madness in the figures of Septimus Warren Smith and Rhoda in *The Waves*. Richard has always fictionalized his friends, employing narrative to populate the hyperbolic world he wanted to live in; "some have ended their relations with him rather than continue as figures in the epic poem he is always composing inside his head, the story of his life and passions" (p.61). As his mental health is destroyed this tendency is exacerbated to the point where he can no longer distinguish the boundaries between himself and his fictions. Woolf's presentation of madness then, which Cunningham develops, is one that is already a feature of creativity. For Woolf this tendency was countered by Leonard's resolute existence in the real world, but Richard Brown's closest support, Clarissa, is apparently all too willing to go along with his dramatizations, even at the end, answering to the name of Mrs. Dalloway; "This is her. I'm her" (p.198).

The insanity of the artist is thus privileged within *The Hours*: as we have seen, Laura's domestic ambitions are elevated through comparison with the processes of writing a novel. This sense is formed by an over-determination of Woolf's own insanity and privileging of the interior monologue at the expense of social critique. In *Mrs. Dalloway* Woolf's diagnosis of Septimus Warren Smith's shellshock has been recognized as "a political reading, ahead of Foucault, of the conspiracy between social engineering, the restraint of the mentally ill, and the patriarchal self-protection of the establishment" (Lee, p.193). In her novel unsympathetic doctors find Smith guilty of a lack of "proportion" and cowardice—they attempt to repress his memories of the death of his fellow soldier and find these remembrances emasculating. There is an absence of figures of social regimentation in *The Hours*. The protagonists who seek oblivion are instead constrained by self-imposed pursuit of artistic perfection. Above all the relationship between Woolf's writing and insanity is magnified. In condensing real biographical events—the station scene—into one day and prefacing the whole day's narrative with her suicide, Cunningham magnifies the intensity and causality of the relationship between creativity and insanity. Woolf did not take her life until some eighteen years later.

Sexuality and narrative

Modernist experimentation in narrative style arose from the desire to represent the flux of consciousness; selfhood as the experience of endlessly contested negotiations between inner and social lives. This project would seem, as Gregory Woods has suggested, germane to the production of "fruitful explorations of deviant states of mind" but in his commanding *History of Gay Literature* he is critical of Woolf's fictions for neglecting the impact of society in her representation of gay experience (Woods, p.202). Focusing on Septimus Warren Smith's ties to Evans, his dead comrade, and the love for Percival that terminally isolates Neville in *The Waves*, he argues instead that she presents male-male desire as so internalized as to result in traumatic lifelong obsessions. He regards her "preoccupation with psychological reality as an excuse for representing love between men as a private affair, so emphatically divorced from the social realm as not to require the definition 'homosexual'" (Woods, p.202).

It is true that we wouldn't look to Woolf for civic realism; she famously elides the First World War in one parenthetical sentence in *To the Lighthouse*, after all. But her admirers, Michael Cunningham among them, would argue that the absence of social realism does not detract from the presentation of the pervasive forces of the public sphere upon the individual consciousness (Canning, N. pag.). Furthermore, to say that Woolf resists categorizations and social labels of any kind in her characterization is not to undermine Woods's point about the particular lack of named homosexuality in her novels, but to suggest instead that her model may be found to be even more fertile to the contemporary writer representing experience at a time when, as we have seen above, we recognize sexuality not as a fixed, definable identity but as a fluid force.

An analysis of focalization in *The Hours* indeed suggests that sexuality is too polymorphous to be determined by fixed labels of identity. The libidinous impulses of the central protagonists whose inner lives are most fully drawn—Woolf, Laura Brown, Clarissa Vaughan and Richard Brown—seem to be the least rigidly demarcated. All have experienced same- and opposite-sex desire. Indeed we might argue that it is precisely because their interiors are more comprehensively revealed that we know their desires to be fluid. There is a narrative implication that were the spotlight to linger on the more marginal characters we might find categorizations of them, as simply straight or gay, too limiting. For instance when Louis Waters— whose only heterosexual experience perversely arose out of a wretched attempt "to retain his claim on Richard" (p.138)—gains momentary control of the narrative we find him "absurdly in love with Julia (he who has never been attracted to women, never)" (p.138). There is however, one avowedly militant homosexual in *The Hours*, Mary Krull, notably presented through the focalization of Clarissa whose envy of Krull's close bond with Julia inevitably colors her depiction. True to her template, she is the least attractive character in the novel. Krull's ugly name and single-faceted political stridency is a duplication of Miss Kilman's rigid adherence to Christian doctrine in *Mrs. Dalloway*. Cunningham's portraits are too tender, however, to let even Mary Krull be denied all compassion. She escapes caricature in the momentary expression of her painfully unrequited desire for Julia who inspires an "erotic patriotism" in her (p.161).

This metaphor echoes Clarissa's meditative justification for rejecting Richard in favor of monogamy with a woman.

Venture too far for love, she tells herself, and you renounce citizenship in the country you've made for yourself. You end up just sailing from port to port. (p.97)

It is a surprising moment of comparison for Clarissa and Mary who personify two apparently competing theoretical perspectives upon lesbian social identity. These longstanding debates are explicitly presented in an imagined exchange between them in which Krull despises "queers of the old school" with their emulation of marriage, of straight society (p.160). Clarissa meanwhile condemns Krull's "self-aggrandizing" stance as merely gestural, seemingly an example of the transgression that Elizabeth Wilson has found insubstantial, rooted only in "a desire to shock" (Bristow, *Activating Theory: Lesbian, Gay, Bisexual Politics*, p.110). Clarissa concludes her diatribe "your hour will come and go" (p.161). She cannot understand why her daughter is attracted to Krull. While to Clarissa's dismay Julia has adopted the sartorial style demanded by Mary's subcultural status, there is no suggestion in the narrative that the appeal for Julia is sexual—nor was there for her counterpart in *Mrs. Dalloway*. Julia's libido is one of the many sexual lacunae in the text. Her mother, meanwhile, following Woolf's narrative—and Cunningham suggests, biographical—precedent has opted for uxoriousness over concupiscence. Clarissa is knowingly prim. It is significant that her life-defining kiss with Richard occurs analeptically.

Despite its seeming chasteness her assimilative marriage is, however, viewed far more sympathetically in *The Hours* than the bitter dogmatism of Mary Krull. Krull's theoretical standpoint seems only further undermined by the implied absence of physical sexual relationships. Rejected by Julia, her libidinous energies have been sublimated instead into the politics of public sexual identity and a censorious hostility to the mainstream, which seems outmoded in the New York society Cunningham depicts. It is only the revelation of Krull's erotic desire that prevents her sexual identity from appearing entirely socially constructed; only this interior glimpse presents an essentialist perspective of her sexuality. Prior to it she is merely a one-dimensional expression of the political belief that sexual identity is not a private matter but bound up with transformation of society. She is alone in this part of the triptych in demanding social change. She regards Clarissa's "marriage" not only as an act of homosexual self-erasure but deluded in believing itself to be socially sanctioned; Mary wants to scream at Clarissa *"You honestly believe that if they come to round up the deviants, they won't stop at your door, don't you?"* (p.160) [original italics].

The closest—significantly absent—parallel to Krull's impassioned, italicized polemic within the text occurs in Clarissa's meditations upon Richard as he was in good health. She misses the arguments they once shared, the wit and political agenda that have been destroyed by his illness. For the deafening subtext of *The Hours* is AIDS. His imminent death and the epidemic silence *all* diatribes. The absence of physical sex similarly finds its explanation within the logic of the diegesis, in the same reason. Unlike Louis, Richard is no longer capable of the pursuit of lovers. And in a telling verb, Evan, the partner of the novel's healthiest body (Walter Hardy) must "husband" his depleted energies for clubbing. Clarissa is thus not alone in favoring uxoriousness; sex has been surmounted by a "capacity for devotion" (p.18). Further explanation for the novel's sublimation of physical sexuality—which surely surprises the readers of Cunningham's previous prose—is again found in the mood of its

template, *Mrs. Dalloway*. Cunningham has combined Woolf's privileging of interiority with her pervasive sense of writing in the aftermath of a devastating event—he parallels the AIDS plague with the
First World War. In these emulations Woods's charge against Woolf
may well thus be leveled at *The Hours*, certainly the novel's most
troubling and transgressive sexual acts remain private and unnamed.

The kiss between Virginia and Vanessa, and Laura and her
neighbor, take place within the novel's earlier historical periods, and
notably occur within the present tenses of the narrative, unlike the
analeptic epiphanies of both Clarissa in *Mrs. Dalloway* and Clarissa
Vaughan. Unlike Laura's bookish and foreign appearance, Kitty has
outwardly seemed to embody American ideals of womanhood and
family values. Her infertility and acquiescence to Laura's desire,
however, belie the simplicity of such concepts. Laura's sense of
being foreign, and a predator, indicates awareness of her transgression, although she avoids the stigmatization of definition by explain-
ing the embrace—like Clarissa Dalloway did—as an experience of
experimental simulacra "This is how a man feels, holding a woman"
(p.109). That it occurs in the present, causing mild anxiety, suggests
a fear of ostracization that has been subsumed by darker terrors in
the later narrative of the 1990s. Virginia Woolf—as a Cunningham
character—too subsumes her transgressive kiss into wider yearnings—for the frissons of metropolitan life. In the narrative depiction
of both transgressions therefore there is acknowledgement that to
name the act as homosexual, and incestuous in the case of Woolf, is
to submit to stigmatization, precisely a recognition of the pressures
of the normative, of the public sphere that Woods found lacking in
Woolf's prose. In his reading of Woolf, Cunningham is explicitly in-
volved in the literary creation of fluid and disruptive identities: his
adaptive expansion to include three narratives charts a historical
progression of absences, from secrecy toward assimilation.

3

The novel's reception

One of the things that's so very gratifying about the particular recognition this book has gotten is what it implies about a broader perspective on human relationships, about the notion that you can write about gay people and straight people and people of all stripes, people who love each other in all sorts of ways, and that it can find a place in the world." ("The Pulitzer Prize for Fiction," www.pbs.org, April 20, 1999)

It is a fitting irony that *The Hours*, a novel about a writer who wins a prestigious award, should be granted two significant literary accolades: the 1999 Pulitzer Prize for Fiction and the PEN/Faulkner Award. Cunningham was moved that his portrayal of three women of ambivalent sexuality, including a British author, should be celebrated within the remit of the Pulitzer, a prize awarded for "distinguished fiction by an American author, preferably dealing with American life" (http://www.pulitzer.org/year/1999/fiction). The PEN/Faulkner prize, established by writers to honor their peers, is testimony to the critical acclaim of fellow novelists. But the American public too has embraced the novel; *The Hours* spent weeks on the best seller lists at the time of publication, after the prizes, and upon release of Stephen Daldry's 2002 film adaptation.

In Britain, however, public recognition of the novel was a little slower. In a 1999 review of novels that failed to perform as expected, Christopher Potter of Fourth Estate described how he hastened the publication of the paperback edition of *The Hours* in the wake of the Pulitzer, and how he was subsequently dismayed at the disappointing sales and lack of media coverage of the prize. His only explanation is a possessive nationalism; "Are we too proprietorial of Virginia Woolf to allow an American to apprehend her?" ("The crackers that failed to go pop," *The Independent*, December 18, 1999). Kate Figes's response is also mindful of Woolf's reputation in Britain; "perhaps the Woolf connection pigeon-holes this book as 'Bloomsbury' rather than general fiction. Those who have never read *Mrs. Dalloway* are bound to be put off" (ibid.). Potter and Figes were rightly dismayed that a book which had been hailed by literary editors and the national press should go so unnoticed among the British public.

On both sides of the Atlantic, however, literary reviewers felt that Cunningham's deployment of a revered figure and emulation of her style was courageous but extraordinarily accomplished. Not just a "party trick"—as Cunningham had feared ("Driving Mrs. Dalloway," *The Guardian*, November 13, 1999)—or a simple updating of her classic but "a delicate, triumphant glance, an acknowledgment of Woolf that takes her into Cunningham's own territory" (Michael Wood, "Parallel Lives," *New York Times*, November 22, 1998). Jonathan Dee, in a review essay for *Harper's* magazine, celebrates *The Hours* as not just a homage to an innovative writer but a paean to the role of literature in our lives; the novel offers "as its animating force that most unfashionable of love objects, a book" ("*The Hours*: Review," *Harper's*, June 1999). Several critics shared this view that Cunningham's achievement was to centralize the importance of fiction, making the "reader believe in the possibility and depth of a communality based on great literature, literature that has shown people how to live and what to ask of life" ("Best '98 Fiction," *Publishers Weekly*). Although *Salon* was a voice of rare dissent amongst the popular press in finding *The Hours* less affecting than *Mrs. Dalloway*, most praised Cunningham not just for directing readers back to Woolf's classic but for reaffirming her significance. There was general agreement that knowledge of *Mrs. Dalloway* was not necessary for enjoyment of *The Hours* but as Michael Wood concludes the connections between the two books "are so rich and subtle and offbeat that not to read *Mrs. Dalloway* after *The Hours* seems like a horrible denial of a readily available pleasure—as if we were to leave a concert just when the variations were getting interesting" (Michael Wood, ibid.).

Unsurprisingly, perhaps, there is some ambivalence among Woolf scholars about Cunningham's prose and story. In the *Woolf Bulletin*—of the Virginia Woolf Society of Great Britain—Linda J. Langham relishes Cunningham's alchemy in satisfying wishes for a "Woolf *nouvelle*," for "genuinely and plausibly return[ing] Woolf's presence" (Linda J. Langham, *Virginia Woolf Bulletin* 3, January 2000, p.67). But although she finds it the most dexterous of three recent novels which take Woolf as their muse (Robin Lippincott, *Mr. Dalloway: A Novella*, 1999, and Sigrid Nunez, *Mitz: The Marmoset of Bloomsbury*, 1998), Karen Levenback employs the words "derivative" and "manipulative" on more than one occasion during her review for the *Woolf Studies Annual* (Volume 6, 2000, pp.198–206). She is surprised that Cunningham did not turn to more primary sources—especially Helen M. Wussow's holograph draft of *Mrs. Dalloway* (1996)—feeling that closer analysis of Woolf's "writing practice" would have been biographically illuminating and furthered his character development. Although she found *The Hours* "strong and resonant" she is particularly critical of "the suicide/sanity motif used by Cunningham to frame his 'character' of Virginia Woolf" (*Woolf Studies Annual*, Volume 6, 2000, p.204). Michael Wood was also doubtful about the weight given to Woolf's suicide in the prologue but for structural reasons: "I thought, until I was a good way into the book, that this beginning was a mistake: too heavy, quite apart from the stylistic risk" (Michael Wood, ibid.). Wood re-evaluated his initial critique in the light of events befalling the other main protagonists; Cunningham's skill in interweaving their three narratives has garnered much applause.

But most praise has been reserved for the luminosity of his prose. Hermione Lee was especially impressed by the depiction of Richard Brown's apartment lobby; Cunningham's "wonderfully textured writing" is "alive with intense observation" ("Mrs. Brown's secret" *The Times Literary Supplement*, August 1 1999). It is "gorgeous, Woolfian, shimmering, perfectly-observed prose" (*Booklist*, September 15, 1998) which amounts to an "elegiac meditation on anger, mistrust, and loneliness" (*Harper's Bazaar*). And while his prose may be "Woolfian," his style has been deemed definably his own (Mel Gussow, "A Writer Haunted by Virginia Woolf" *New York Times*, April 20 1999). Critics familiar with Cunningham's earlier novels note the economy of his prose in *The Hours*; it is prismatic rather than expansive. These qualities led several critics to share the view of Robert Plunkett; "best of all, it's a real book. It could never, ever be a movie" ("Imagining Woolf," *The Advocate*, December 8 1998).

·** 4**

The Novel on Film

It's unsurprising that many critics felt that *The Hours* could not be translated into a film. The novel of interior monologues, intertextuality, the relationship between authors, fictions, readers, has a modernist text at its emotional and structural centre. How could fears of frailty, the value of reading *Mrs. Dalloway* be represented on screen? What could replace the enactment of authorship?

In fact the film (Miramax / Paramount, 2002) implicitly perpetuates the staging of Woolf as its author. There are moments from *Mrs. Dalloway* that don't appear in Cunningham's novel: like Clarissa Dalloway, but not Vaughan, Laura Brown observes a removal van at her neighbors'. More significantly in focusing upon the role and representation of Woolf, reviews of the film have located issues of authorship with her. Stephen Daldry, the film's director, countered criticisms of its portrayal of Woolf, with admiration for the film's achievement in propelling *Mrs. Dalloway* into the top ten US fiction best-sellers chart (a sidelining of the similar fortunes of Cunningham's novel). Hostile to what he perceives as the nitpicking of British academics, Daldry polarizes the film's critical reception in a celebration of the US public's embracing of the canonical text

(*Open Book*, Radio 4, February 16, 2003). The depiction of Woolf by Nicole Kidman has become the key issue of the film's reviews. Consequently Cunningham's authorship is once again erased. Instead he can be glimpsed for a second on a Manhattan street, beaming as he walks past Clarissa Vaughan on her way to the flower shop. No doubt amused by this in-joke, Cunningham's momentary and uncredited appearance allows him to enter his fiction, both asserting his authorial agency and denying his visibility as author. In his novel and Woolf's the Clarissa characters encounter acquaintances and passers by as they perambulate their city streets whilst in the film, Clarissa Vaughan exchanges and overhears no conversation, and is only encountered by her anonymous creator.

Daldry did not perceive the formal qualities of the novel as a barrier to transformation for a visual medium; the triptych was "a wonderful opportunity to try to create a single narrative" ("About the Production" *The Hours* Screening Notes, 16). For BBC Radio 4's Tom Sutcliffe the film is thus a thriller; Daldry has supplied visual clues as to how the lives of the three women fit together. The motifs of flowers and an egg being broken upon the rim of a bowl occur in each of their days. Although each story has a different color palette, costume features are handed down; Clarissa's earrings resemble Woolf's; Richie (Jack Rovello)'s bedspread becomes Richard (Ed Harris)'s dressing gown. Equally, the composed score of Philip Glass underlines their commonality of experience—over-insistently according to Adam Mars-Jones—he deliberately chose to have one theme for this effect, rather than three distinct signature melodies. This forms a parallel to the novel's formal and syntactical repetitions. There is a further visual acknowledgement of both novels' prose representation of the indivisibility of lives in the film's opening and closing sequence of Woolf's graceful and sunlit submission into a fertile and endlessly flowing river.

However, film is a visual and aural format and those who were most doubtful of the adaptation of *The Hours* from page to celluloid were those most impressed by the primacy of *Mrs. Dalloway* as a formal structure, and the power of reading, in Cunningham's novel. The interiority of text disappears in the adaptation in two significant ways. Firstly, reading disappears. In the film books appear as offering only trait connotation for the spectator; Laura Brown's estrangement from American family life is signified clearly to her neighbor and her husband through her love of books; it is a sign of oddness and isolation. No longer a source of solace and respite, instead *Mrs. Dalloway* inspires thoughts of suicide in her. She escapes home to the hotel not to read in tranquility but, emptying the contents of her drug cabinet into her handbag, to commit suicide, in an altogether hysterical departure from her screaming son and "ridiculous car scene" (Karen Wright, *Saturday Review* Radio 4, Saturday 15, 2003). Richard Brown's novel, tantalizingly given a half-glimpsed title — *The _____ of Time* — is merely the motivation for Clarissa's party, and a shortcut expression of the history of their relationship.

Secondly, and most profoundly, the interior monologues of the three women are translated into outward expression or visual forms. "In film, you can't have inner voice unless you have voiceover. We made a very specific decision at the very beginning not to have voiceover" observed David Hare, the screenwriter for *The Hours*. Clearly, three interwoven voiceovers would have betrayed the format of film, not to mention been tedious and potentially confusing, but Hare's consequent adaptation of much interior thought to dialogue is problematic. It overturns the delicate sensibilities of the novel especially in the characterization of Laura Brown (Julianne Moore) and Clarissa Vaughan (Meryl Streep). As discussed above, in the novel Laura frets over the amateurishness of the birthday cake she makes for her husband (John C. Reilly), regarding it as metonymically indicative of her wider failure in her maternal and marital roles. In the film, however, this "failure" is externally witnessed and recognized by Kitty (Toni Collette) who brashly declares upon seeing it that "Anyone can bake a cake" as if to point out that Laura is visibly inadequate. The power structure is similarly inverted in Clarissa's meeting with Louis Waters (Jeff Daniels). In the novel she is afforded a small inner satisfaction in finding Louis's latest love affair with his much younger, ruggedly-named, student Hunter Craydon, derisory. This becomes accusatory in the film when Louis asks Clarissa; "You think I'm ridiculous?" In fact Hare has switched their roles and relationship entirely; Louis is apparently not ridiculous, nor even sentimental: it is Clarissa who breaks down and not Louis who slips off to the fountain for a few mawkish tears.

The adaptation from private meditation to musings out loud presents both mothers, Laura and Clarissa, as at best callous, at worst cruel. The tyres on Laura's car screech as she leaves her inconsolable son screaming whilst Clarissa actually tells Julia (Claire Danes) that her only moment of happiness occurred long before her daughter's birth. Despite Daldry's claims that for him the essence of *The Hours* "is its profound respect for women" and their stoicism (*The Hours* Screening Notes, 17), Cherry Potter has claimed that his film makes monsters of the women, engendering sympathy instead for their long-suffering sons, husbands, and lovers (*Back Row*, BBC Radio 4, February 15, 2003). One of the film's very few flashbacks tells that Richard Brown throws himself to his death not because he fears he has failed as an artist, nor indeed that he is dying painfully from an AIDS-related illness, but because his mother left him as a child.

This further denial of the centrality of writing and artistic achievement of Cunningham's novel may, according to Adam Mars-Jones, be attributable to the medium. He rightly points out that "movies have difficulties with artists;" in Kidman's Woolf "artistic endeavor comes across as a series of frowns" (*Saturday Review* Radio 4, Saturday 15, 2003). Criticism of the portrayal of Woolf has thus not been entirely located in Kidman's Oscar-winning performance but also in the biographical inaccuracies and over-emphasis on the fragility of her mental health which partly originate in Cunningham's novel itself. Although rising to hysteria in the scene at Richmond Station, some have charged Kidman's Woolf with a vagueness and abstraction which runs counter to her reputation as a wit and lover of parties, London, and the social scene. Her relationship with Leonard (Stephen Dillane) is more of imprisonment than in the novel; he is depicted as her jailer not her stalwart and beloved defender. Their companionship delicately depicted by Cunningham in their shared joke about Nelly's (over) cooking as they walk home from the station having agreed to move back to London, is replaced in the film by Leonard's stern assertion that Nelly has had "a difficult day" and so they must return for dinner. He is placed on the side of the cook, of propriety and not within an intimate bond with his wife. As with the failure to present uxoriousness between Sally and Clarissa Vaughan—at the film's start Sally seems to return from a night's infidelity to Clarissa's bed—"capacity for devotion" is rather fiercely administered in Daldry's film. The portrayal of domesticity and coupledom seems relentlessly grim.

The film has, however, won awards and much critical acclaim. The accomplished casting secured sensitive performances from those playing the smaller as well as key roles. When Dan leaves for work and Laura is alone with Richie, Moore's look as she turns from the window to her small son is bestowed with an almost unbearably poignant fragility and terror as she faces the day ahead as his mother. Whilst critics have variously nominated each of the three main actors for the most accolades there has been a universal, often risible, preoccupation with Kidman's prosthetic nose. In applauding and focusing upon her transfiguration from 21st century star to dowdy modernist, the film forgets the intertextuality and author-text relationship of *The Hours* for the intermediality of the actor's relationship to her role.

Further reading and discussion questions

Questions for discussion

1. Michael Wood has said that the connections between Cunningham's novel and Woolf's "are so rich and subtle and offbeat that not to read *Mrs. Dalloway* after *The Hours* seems like a horrible denial of a readily available pleasure." In what ways is the novel enhanced by knowledge of Virginia Woolf's modernist classic?

2. The "Mrs. Woolf" chapters of *The Hours* might be termed "biographical fiction." Does Cunningham's insertion of Woolf's domestic concerns into the writing of her novel transform a reading of *Mrs. Dalloway*?

3. In his interview with Richard Canning, Cunningham describes the novel he is currently working on as another literary triptych, featuring Walt Whitman in each of the three narratives. Which aspects of Virginia Woolf's life has Cunningham chosen to emphasize through his fictionalization of her in *The Hours*?

4. To write about gay characters "is always, necessarily, to make some sort of 'statement' about the fact of being gay" (David Leavitt). In what ways might *The Hours* be categorized a "gay novel"?

5. Do you agree with Reed Woodhouse that Cunningham does not overturn the strong mother/weak father etiology asserted by Irving Bieber to be the "cause" of homosexual sons? How far is Richard Brown's life depicted as being shaped by his relationship with his mother, Laura Brown?

6. Although Clarissa Vaughan has more personal and social freedom than either Virginia Woolf or Laura Brown, she has become a fairly conventional wife and mother. What does the narrative indicate about motherhood; does it suggest it is a biologically-determined drive or a role that society still demands of women?

7. As in *Mrs. Dalloway*, insanity seems to be connected to creativity in *The Hours*. What does the novel imply about the nature of insanity? And how is it connected to the social roles each character is called upon to play?

8. Aside from narrative coherence in the interweaving of the three women's lives, what is the significance of the motif of the yellow roses? What do they mean to Virginia Woolf, Laura Brown and Clarissa Vaughan, and to the "spouses" who offer them?

9. What is the importance of London, Los Angeles and New York City to the main characters?

10. Woolf's working title for *Mrs. Dalloway* was "The Hours." What is the significance of time, "the hours" to each of the main protagonists in Cunningham's novel? Why has he chosen to depict their lives through just one day?

11. After meditating on memories of youth, Clarissa concludes that a moment of happiness with Richard and Louis at Wellfleet was in fact a defining moment in her life. How does the narrative depict Clarissa and Richard as shaping their lives around memory?

12. Do you feel that the parallel between the aftermath of World War I (in *Mrs. Dalloway*) and the era of the AIDS epidemic (in *The Hours*) is successfully drawn?

Bibliography

SELECTED WORKS BY MICHAEL CUNNINGHAM

Longer works

Golden States. New York: Crown, 1981.

A Home at the End of the World. New York: Farrar, Straus & Giroux, 1990. Edition Used. Harmondsworth: Penguin, 1991.

Flesh and Blood. New York: Farrar, Straus and Giroux, 1995. Edition Used. Harmondsworth: Penguin, 1996.

The Hours. New York: Farrar, Straus and Giroux, 1998. Edition Used. London: Fourth Estate, 1999.

Land's End: A Walk Through Provincetown. New York: Crown Journeys, 2002.

Short stories

"Bedrock" *Redbook* (April 1981).

"Clean Dreams" *Wigwag* (August 1990); and Ravenel, Shannon & Atwood, Margaret Eleanor eds. *Best American Short Stories 1989.* New York: Houghton Mifflin, 1989; and Mordden, Ethan ed. *Waves: an Anthology of New Gay Fiction.* New York: Vintage, 1994.

"Cleaving" *Atlantic* (January 1991).
"Mister Brother" *DoubleTake*, 14 (1999).
"Pearls" *Paris Review* (Fall 1982).
"The Slap of Love" *Open City#6* (www.opencity.org).
"White Angel" *The New Yorker* (July 25 1988).

Critical studies

"First Love" *PEN-America*, 1.1 (Winter 2000), 34–35.
"On Contemporary Gay Male Literature in the United States." Martin Duberman ed. *Queer Representations: Reading Lives, Reading Cultures.* New York: New York UP, 1997.
"Thinking about Fabulousness" in Robert Vorlicky ed. *Tony Kushner in Conversation.* Ann Arbor: University of Michigan Press, 1998.
Introd. Stadler, Matthew. *The Dissolution of Nicholas Dee: His Researches.* New York: Grove Press, 2000.
Introd. Woolf, Virginia. *The Voyage Out.* Modern Library Edition, New York: Random House, 2000. Edited version at www.salon.com/books/feature/2000/06/22/woolf/story.jpg

SELECT CRITICISM

Works on gay fiction
Bergman, David. *Gaiety Transfigured: Gay Self-Representation in American Literature.* Madison: University of Wisconsin Press, 1991.
Brookes, Les. *Gay Male Writing Since Stonewall,* unpublished PhD thesis, 2003.
Leavitt, David and Mitchell, Mark intro and eds. *The Penguin Book of Gay Short Stories.* Harmondsworth: Penguin, 1994.
Weeks, Jeffrey. *Coming Out: Homosexual Politics in Britain, from the Nineteenth Century to the Present.* London: Quartet, 1990.
Woods, Gregory. *A History of Gay Literature: The Male Tradition.* New Haven: Yale UP, 1998.

Works on or connected with The Hours

Coffey, Michael. "Michael Cunningham: New Family Outings." *Publisher's Weekly*. 254.44 (November 2 1998), 53–55.

Cunningham, Michael. "For 'The Hours,' an Elation Mixed With Doubt," *New York Times*, (January 19 2003).

Dee, Jonathan. "The Hours. Review Essay." *Harper's*, June 1999.

Gussow, Mel. "A Writer Haunted by Virginia Woolf," *New York Times*, (April 20 1999).

Guthman, Edward. "Dancing with Woolf," *Advocate*, (Sept 15 1998).

Johnston, Sheila. "A Day in the Life." *Sight & Sound*, February 2003, 24–7.

Lane, Christopher. "When Plagues Don't End." *Gay and Lesbian Review Worldwide*, 8.1 (Jan–Feb 2001), 30–32.

Lee, Hermione. "Mrs. Brown's Secret" (Book Review). *The Times Literary Supplement*, (August 1 1999), 13.

Langham, Linda J. "The Hours" (Book Review). *Virginia Woolf Bulletin*, Volume 3 (January 2000), 67–69.

Levenback, Karen L. "The Hours" (Book Review). *Woolf Studies Annual*, Volume 6 (2000), 198–206.

Plunkett, Robert. "Imagining Woolf" (Book Review). *The Advocate*, (December 8 1998).

Spring, Justin. "Michael Cunningham." *BOMB*, 66 (Winter 1999), 76–80.

Wolf, Matt. "Clarissa Dalloway in a Hall of Mirrors," *New York Times*, (November 3 2002).

Wood, Michael. "Parallel Lives" (Book Review). *New York Times*, (November 22 1998).

Wroe, Nicholas. "Driving Mrs. Dalloway" (Book Review). *The Guardian*, (November 13 1999).

On Michael Cunningham and his other works

Canning, Richard. *Hear Me Out: Further Conversations with Gay Novelists*. New York: Columbia UP, 2003.

Eder, Richard. "Squaring a Triangle." *Los Angeles Times Book Review*, (November 11 1990), 3.

Jarraway, David R. "'The Novel That Took the Place of a Poem': Wallace Stevens and Queer Discourse." *English Studies in Canada*, 22.4 (December 1996), 377–97.

Kaufman, David. "All in the Family." *The Nation*, (July 1 1991), 21.

Kornblatt, Joyce Reiser. "Such Good Friends." *New York Times Book Review*, (November 11 1990), 12.

Nealon, Chris. "Get a Life." *Gay Community News*, (August 4–10 1991), 8.

Olshan, Joseph. "Two trips through the minefields of emotions." *Chicago Tribune Book Review*, (November 4 1990), 8.

Stambolian, George. "Searching for Sensibilities." *The Advocate*, (October 23 1990), 74.

Woodhouse, Reed. *Unlimited Embrace: A Canon of Gay Fiction, 1945–1995*. Amherst: University of Massachusetts Press, 1998.

Woodhouse, Reed. *Michael Cunningham (1952–   )*. Emmanuel S. Nelson ed., *Contemporary Gay American Novelists: A Bio-Bibliographical Critical Sourcebook*. Westport, Connecticut: Greenwood, 1993.

Websites on Michael Cunningham

Reading and Conversation, November 14, 2001, www.lannan.org
www.literati.net/Cunningham/index.htm
http://www.barclayagency.com/cunningham.html
http://www.english.upenn.edu/~whfellow/whfellowinfo.html#cunningham

SELECTED WORKS BY VIRGINIA WOOLF

Jacob's Room, London: Hogarth Press, 1922.

Mrs. Dalloway. London: Hogarth Press, 1925. Edition Used. Oxford: Oxford UP, 1992.

Orlando. London: Hogarth Press, 1928.

A Room of One's Own, London: Hogarth Press, 1929.

To the Lighthouse, London: Hogarth Press, 1927.

The Waves, London: Hogarth Press, 1931.

Bell, Anne Olivier. *The Diary of Virginia Woolf Volume II: 1920–24*. London: Hogarth Press, 1978.

Dick, Susan ed. *Complete Shorter Fiction*. London: Triad Grafton Books, 1991.

McNeillie, Andrew. *The Essays of Virginia Woolf: Volume 3: 1919 to 1924*. London: Hogarth Press, 1998.

SELECTED WORKS ON VIRGINIA WOOLF AND *MRS. DALLOWAY*

Boone, Joseph. *Libidinal Currents: Sexuality and the Shaping of Modernism*. Chicago: University of Chicago Press, 1998.

Lee, Hermione. *Virginia Woolf*. London: Chatto & Windus, 1996.

Marcus, Laura. *Auto/Biographical Discourses: Criticism, Theory, Practice*. Manchester: Manchester UP, 1994.

Showalter, Elaine. *The Female Malady: Women, Madness and English Culture, 1830–1980*. London: Virago Press, 1987.

Snaith, Anna. *Virginia Woolf: Public and Private Negotiations*. Basingstoke: Macmillan, 2000.

Woolf, Leonard. *Downhill All the Way: An Autobiography of the Years 1919 to 1939*. London: Hogarth Press, 1967.

Wussow, Helen M. trans. and ed. *Virginia Woolf "The Hours": The British Museum Manuscript of Mrs. Dalloway*. New York: Pace UP, 1996.

Wyatt, Jean. "Avoiding Self-Definition: In Defense of Women's Right to Merge (Julia Kristeva and *Mrs. Dalloway*)." *Women's Studies: An Interdisciplinary Journal*, 13. 1–2 (1986), 115–126.